BRIGHT YOUNG THINGS

© 2000 Assouline
Photographs © 2000 Jonathan Becker

Assouline Publishing
601 West 26th Street
18th floor
New York, NY 10001
USA

www.assouline.com

ISBN: 2 84323 205 8

Printed in Italy

Brooke de Ocampo

BRIGHT YOUNG THINGS

Photographs by Jonathan Becker

Interviews by Shax F. Riegler

ASSOULINE

For Ines, Isabel and Marina, my sweet angels,
and Emilio, for his love and encouragement.

CONTENTS

INTRODUCTION

A period of extended prosperity has opened the playing fields in New York City to a new, young group: the Bright Young Things.

From hip music stars to beauty business tycoonesses, these meritocrats—don't call them aristocrats—are dressing the town with their notions of chic and cool. Exceedingly influential, they speak the new language of Style with sounds, and symbols, that signify a global mix, the worlds of interior design and fashion constantly melding. Why care about Manhattan's Bright Young Things? Because New York is the laboratory for the New International Style, and style is the great medium of the moment. "Style" is shorthand in fast times, flashcards against towering babble.

Decoration, like clothing, as the fashion historian James Laver wrote, "is inevitable. They are nothing less than the furniture of the mind made visible." By the way they wear clothes, decorate, and collect, New York's Bright Young Things (BYTs) define a new social order organized around the privileges of meritocracy, not aristocracy.

"People with money and taste are always welcome in New York," Brooke Astor declared to *W* not long ago.

Bright Young Things practice the stylish politics of inclusion, instead of exclusion. Post-feminist, and post-assorted other essential liberation movements, the message is: be yourself, but be very good at it. Work hard. Play hard. And no one gentrifies anymore. BYTs are too busy changing their clothes, mixing a Gap T-shirt with a Bill Blass ballgown skirt, or turning a seven-room Park Avenue co-op into a Downtown-like loft space. For New York's new meritocrats, the language of style, its varying codes of status, its symbols and shorthands, is way more compelling than an almanac written in blue blood. "Style" is the New Club. *Vogue, W, Harper's Bazaar, Vanity Fair,* and *Elle Decor,* among other publications, are the new Social Registers, tallying glossies that chronicle the way today's Bright Young Things live and shop.

The idea for this book came to Brooke de Ocampo, a former *Vogue* editor now contributing to *Harper's Bazaar*—and card-carrying BYT herself—last year when she was reading an out-of-print edition of *Vogue's Book of Houses, Gardens, People* first published in 1963. People like Madame Jacques Balsan (Consuelo Vanderbilt), Doris Duke, Pauline de Rothschild, Amanda and Carter Burden, Nancy Lancaster, and Emilio Pucci were photographed by Horst at home, in the splendor of their day. "Few things are more fascinating than the opportunity to see how other people live during their private hours—in the rooms they love, in the gardens they have planted, among their personal possessions, pursuing their favorite interests, enjoying their special comforts, organizing their domestic arrangements to fit the pattern of their individual lives," Diana Vreeland wrote in her introduction to the book.

"But that was a certain era, another time," Brooke de Ocampo observed when she and the photographer Jonathan Becker were shooting the stories for this book in the year 2000. "Style was noticed on a much more elite group. Now it really is about the Mix. There are so many different people from so many different backgrounds—anything goes in the city today. And personal style, not authorities dictating what is acceptable taste, is the rule, not the exception, in everything from what these people wear, to what they eat, where they vacation, and how they do their interiors. What I really notice is how much the Bohemian, or the idea of the Bohemian, influences the way the people decorate now."

Good news, bad news? The Bohemian and the Bourgeois are all mixed together nowadays, a result of the hedonism of the Beats in the 1950s, the rebellion of the Hippies in the 1960s, and advanced by the motivational "Me" generation self-actualizers in the 1970s who wrenched the heights of capitalism away from the aristocrats and gave it to a new, vast class of educated, adamant achievers. And, besides, Bohemians have more fun: which party would you rather attend, Picasso's or your grandfather's banker's?

Bohemian overtures play in the rooms of New York's BYTs. The fondness for flea market treasures, for brightly-colored walls and fabrics, open-space eat-in kitchens, loft spaces and, in general, the BYT pastiche approach to decorating: anything goes as long as it is comfortable, the very best, the most cool, or the most kitschy.

"Everyone who walks in here says it doesn't feel like New York. It feels very Asian," exclaims Peggy Stephaich Guinness, a jewelry designer and Mellon banking heiress, about her loft in SoHo. "It's a real combination of our collections," comments her husband, Sebastian Guinness. "It's pretty Victorian in taste at the moment—full of stuff."

It's the way of the world these days, the "Salad Spinner Effect" as the designer John Bartlett says, in which anything goes as long as the standard is highly evolved and considered. A Saarinen side table keeps company with the ladder from a fire engine in musician Moby's loft. In the loft of Audra Avizienis and Jason Duchin, son of society bandleader Peter Duchin, black-and-white prints from Lithuania, where Audra's parents migrated from, are at home with masks from Bali.

"I desperately need a place where I can relax and not panic," the artist Damian Loeb explains, talking about his Downtown loft where the most important objet is his stereo and the oldest possession is his teddy bear. "I need comfort, protection, privacy, and a place to scream," Loeb says.

"You don't have to tiptoe around this apartment," says Eliza Reed Bolen about the Upper East Side apartment she and husband Alexander Bolen have decorated. "You can sit in here and relax, have a pizza and rent a video, which we do quite regularly. It's not 'fancy,' but it is not full of futons either. It's the way we envision our life and our family to be one day."

"The biggest tension, to put it in the grandest terms, is between worldly success and inner virtue," David Brooks writes in his potent book, *BOBOS [Bourgeois Bohemians] in Paradise: The New Upper Class and How They Got There.* "How do you move ahead in life without letting ambition wither your soul? How do you accumulate the resources you need to do the things you want without becoming a slave to material things? How do you build a comfortable and stable life for your family without getting bogged down in stultifying routine? How do you live at the top of society without becoming an insufferable snob? ... The grand achievement of the educated elites in the 1990s was to create a way of living that lets you be an affluent success and at the same time a free-spirit rebel."

New York's Bright Young Things, like their compatriots in cities around the country, struggle to find the sacred in the profane, the fun in the business suit, the redemption in the chiffon, the meaning in the sofa or table found at a flea market. It can be exhausting. In generations past, Bright Young Things, according to their biographers, stayed out all-night and recuperated all morning, rising to the challenges of luncheon, manners, and trends. The 18th century Georgina, the Duchess of Devonshire. Brenda Frazier in the earlier part of the 20th century. Contemporary BYTs work all day, at something, from dotcoms to dotted conglomerates, and then go out at night, having a social life that, more times than not, is related to the business life of a friend. A preview party at Christie's or Sotheby's. A charity event chaired by a pal. A store opening, followed by dinner at Moomba into the wee hours. Exhausting, but everyone does it, society by night, work by day. (Well, almost everyone works. The others consult.)

"The Nan Kempners of the world," the fashion designer Josh Patner of the dress house Tuleh, a BYT favorite, told fashion writer Cathy Horyn recently, "float on clouds." But today's BYTs, in Patner's opinion, put their "heels to the pavement."

The expression Bright Young Things was coined to define a celebrated London group, including assorted Mitford sisters, Diana Cooper, and Evelyn Waugh, who were "a moment of iconoclastic pleasure-seeking sandwiched between the grim memories of the First World War and the growing economic Depression of the 1930s," as a biographer of the Mitford sisters recently observed. The mothers of today's BYT invention were a formative, and influential group of certain women who, as BYTs in the early 1960s, joined forces with the America's happening fashion designers and, hitched together to the same sartorial star, rose in the imaginations of an adoring public eager to read all about how pearls twirled, so to speak, in Jet Set orbit.

There was Babe Paley, C.Z. Guest, Slim Keith, Gloria Guinness, Marella Agnelli in Europe, Lee Radziwill, Jacqueline Kennedy Onassis, Gloria Vanderbilt—some of whom Truman Capote nicknamed "The Swans." These Ladies fascinated by keeping mostly to their own, individual style path, defining their look and setting trends. On the other hand, Chessy Rayner, Mica Ertegun, Pat Buckley, and Nan Kempner, among others ladies, functioned more as a team as they befriended designing gentlemen such as Bill Blass and Oscar de la Renta. Mica, Chessy, Pat, and Nan wore Bill's and Oscar's designs and, in those wonderful new American clothes, opened the doors of their perfect houses to the late fashion columnist Eugenia Sheppard, to Aileen "Suzy" Mehle, as well as to *Vogue*, the *Bazaar* and, later, *W* until the initially foreign worlds of Park Avenue and Seventh Avenue became eternally, and profitably, bonded.

While Mrs. Buckley and Mrs. Kempner toiled more than full-time on the charity circuit, Mrs. Rayner and Mrs. Ertegun opened an interior design firm, Mac II, in 1965. Mrs. Rayner had been an editor at *Vogue*, and Mrs. Ertegun recently had completed a course of study in interior design. "There aren't any two girls in New York with more on-the-ball, more of a flair for houses, for food, for clothes, for living—than Mica and Chessy," Bill Blass told *Vogue* in 1972.

Girls? "You see how much dignity we command," Chessy Rayner responded at the time. The 1970s saw a sea change for women, even so-called society women. Its impact has had a lasting effect on New York style. Suddenly, work became the proper way a lady, or a well-heeled bachelor, spent their time.

"Whether because of the recession, inflation, Vietnam, campus unrest, the desire to get closer to nature, a new introspection or simply boredom with the old extravagances, a new life style is emerging ... spaghetti parties for eight are replacing formal black-tie dinners for 24," Charlotte Curtis observed in *The New York Times* in 1970.

"We've all changed," Chessy Rayner told Curtis. "That giddy racing around is gone. It's a reaction to what's happening. If you're giddy now, you're insensitive to the world's problems."

Sensitivity to the world's problems, or its facsimile, political correctness combined with the premium put on corporate professionalism, prompted New York society to contain its most frivolous flings to the charity circuit throughout the yuppified 1980s and early 1990s. Acting grown-up was the mandate during the Reagan/Bush era here. The only people who appeared to swing during the 1980s were the artists Downtown, the late Keith Haring, Andy Warhol, Jean-Michel Basquiat. Trendy restaurants, the location for so many expense account dinners, replaced discos and clubs. Meanwhile, today's BYTs were still at school binging on nostaglia for things past, but not too past: the optimistic 1970s that looked like so much fun. Color, pattern, slim, trim, Gucci, Pucci ... lots of laughs if you didn't know these clothes during Vietnam, post-Pill, pre-Betty Ford Clinic and Studio 54.

Of course, according to some seasoned observers, today's BYTs, in their Millenial Gyspy jeans and curried houses, seriously lack the classic glamour of ladies and gentlemen past. "But there aren't any swans," a veteran member of the International Best-Dressed List was heard to opine not long ago, referring to the Marella Agnellis and the Babe Paleys of almost half a century ago.

"It is always a danger to bemoan the lost glories of the past and the barbarism of the present," Cecil Beaton wrote in *The Glass of Fashion*, published in 1954. "If every age is a birth and a dying, better to be on the side of the living than the dead ... Fashion is the subtle and shifting expression of every age ... The important thing, in the last analysis, is whether that image really corresponds to what we feel ourselves to be."

How could there be swans today? The social waters are all sea change, fast and faster, tough on swans, and the tides, and the sands along the way, are constantly shifting between the twin forces of the current season: optimism and futility.

The BYTs aren't swans, no. Instead, as the age commands, they are social sailors, negotiating modern gods and sirens in an odyssey of personal style on the treasured island of Manhattan.

William Norwich

PETER BACANOVIC

Peter Bacanovic, a born and bred New Yorker, lives in the very brownstone on New York's Upper East Side that was the setting for *Breakfast at Tiffany's*, the Audrey Hepburn film that even today epitomizes New York glamour. It's a strange responsibility he's taken on. "I never realized what a cult movie it was until I moved here. People stand outside the apartment and stare. They'll ask if it looks the same inside as it did in the movie." Seasonally he hangs and removes the old-fashioned, green awnings that gave the house its distinctive look in the film.

For a long time, the place belonged to some very good friends. Peter had always admired it and asked them to tell him immediately if it ever became available. One day, the friends called and said, "Peter, we've got good news and bad news. The good news is that we've found a spot that you'll love, the bad news is that it's our apartment—we're getting divorced and you have to give us your decision in 24 hours." Having lived on the 42nd floor of an ultra-modern high-rise, Peter was immediately drawn to the privacy of a brownstone and the luxury of not having to deal with elevators, overstaffed buildings, and neighbors down the hall. In essence, he moved from one extreme to another, from an apartment where the outside view was the dominating factor, to an interior space where the rooms themselves were all-important. "And best of all," claims Peter, "I love being eye-to-eye with the trees, coming down from the clouds I once lived among."

Just as it did in the movie, the house serves as the perfect backdrop for a life that could only exist in New York. As a child of the city, the naturally gregarious Peter has a lifetime's worth of acquaintances to keep up with, and has earned a reputation as a man about town. In addition, as a private banker, he devotes much of his time to his clients—"26 hours a day," he says.

Previous page: Peter Bacanovic on the stoop of his Upper East Side brownstone where the movie *Breakfast at Tiffany's*, starring Audrey Hepburn, was filmed.
Left: Fresh spring tulips on the mantle in the study. A double portrait of Tina Chow by photographer David Seidner sits beside prints found in London and a tulip study by Dethore whose work is in the permanent collection of the Metropolitam Museum of Art.
Above: A Nabil Nahas painting, entitled "PC88," hangs in the living room above a French 1940s ottoman upholstered in chocolate colored pony skin. The small side table is Chinese.
Next page: Peter in his study, which he also uses as a dining room for entertaining. The walls are painted key lime green.

The Bacanovic rooms are painted in soothing yet unexpected shades. Spaces flow easily into each other. Look on any shelf or table and one sees a grouping of framed snapshots—an array of faces from New York's social scene. The small, pale green parlor off the living room is hung with images inspired by *Don Quixote*, his favorite book. Spread throughout the house is his collection of rare fashion illustrations.

Peter's bedroom passion is flowers, images of flowers everywhere. Over his bed hangs one of artist Peter Dayton's large, colorful, distinctive photo-flower collages, with zinnias bursting to the very edge. "I tell people that's what the inside of my head looks like in the morning. Really, it's the happiest thing I've ever seen," Peter says of the painting. Among the other flo ral images is a panel of wallpaper designed by Andy Warhol that the artist presented to him on his 21st birthday, and a charming portrait of Peter as a floral bouquet done by another artist and friend.

"You've got to let a little humor shine through," says Peter when asked about style in dress and decor. "There should always be something to make you smile."

What do you regard as the lowest depth of misery?
Having a serious illness or a destructive dry cleaner.

What is your idea of earthly happiness?
Health, sunny weather, and a suite at the Ritz in Paris.

To what weaknesses are you most indulgent?
Hyperactivity and dissipation.

Who is your favorite painter?
Cy Twombly, all Fauve artists.

What is your favorite virtue?
Generosity—willingness to pick up a check!

What is the quality you most admire in a man?
Directness, strength, pragmatism, warmth.

Who is your favorite writer?
Flaubert, Lewis Carroll, Dr. Seuss, Homere, Cervantes.

What is your favorite occupation?
Caring for sick animals and closing business deals!

What is your most marked characteristic?
Blind optimism.

What is your principle defect?
Blind optimism.

What do you most value in your friends?
Sincerity, consistency, humor, guest rooms.

What to your mind would be the greatest of misfortunes?
For one's child to predecease you and male pattern baldness.

ELIZA REED BOLEN AND ALEX BOLEN

Eliza and Alex Bolen can barely shut their apartment door before being tackled by Emma and Fred, their Glen of Imaal terriers, a rare dog breed from Ireland's mountainous County Wicklow. It's been a long day, but the dogs are thrilled to see them and full of energy. So Eliza and Alex toss their bags in the foyer and get down on the floor for a few minutes of rough-housing before dinner. The dogs are indulged children and definitely have the run of the house. Their beds sit in the middle of the den. Rubber chew toys lie under antique tables and chairs, and stepping on something that squeaks is a regular hazard.

The couple moved into the Upper East Side apartment just after their wedding in 1998. While single, both lived in classic Greenwich Village flats—tiny one-bedrooms that grew crammed over the years. Eliza had inherited many pieces from her family and Alex had been buying antiques and paintings in shops and at auctions for years.

Although their apartment is filled with many grand old things, Eliza and Alex take a decidedly comfortable approach to life. They like to tell the story of how they met over hot dogs and a video game while students at Brown University. The courtship continued after graduation when both moved to Manhattan to pursue their careers. Alex went to Wall Street and Eliza spent four years working with environmental-protection groups before joining her stepfather, fashion designer Oscar de la Renta. A decade later, a similar sense of easygoing informality and welcome pervades the home they have made together—led, of course, by the dogs.

"The hardest room in the house to paint was our bedroom," Eliza begins, surveying her apartment and describing the burnt orange color on the bedroom walls. "I took the color from a ticket stub to a museum in Europe. It took the painters many, many tries but they managed to get it. Now I always want a bedroom this color; it's so warm. When we move we're going to have to cut a chunk of the wall and have it matched. We didn't write down the formula and we lost the ticket stub."

David Netto, an interior designer, helped them edit their choices and pull everything together into a warm and livable space. "You don't have to tiptoe around this apartment," says Eliza. "You can sit in here and relax, have a pizza and rent a video, which we do quite regularly. It's not fancy, but it's not full of futons either. It's the way we envision our life and our family to be one day."

One of the main attractions of this apartment was its large dining area. "The minute Alex saw the room, he had very strong opinions about the way he wanted it to look," Eliza recalls. "Since I had definite ideas for the bedroom, I just let him have the dining room to do with as he pleased. He loves playing the host."

Alex had the room papered with a grisaille mural depicting the Italian countryside. "My grandmother in West Virginia had an old-fashioned dining room with scenic wallpaper and I just had to have something like it here. I feel like I finally get to sit at the grown-ups' table."

Previous page: Eliza Reed Bolen in a red Oscar de la Renta pantsuit seated in the dining room doorway. Alex Bolen in the background playing with dogs, Fred and Emma.

Above, left: Bookshelves in the dining room hold Eliza and Alex's overflowing collection of books along with a large silver plate, a wedding gift. Alex found the English regency globe at auction.

Above, right: A silver box inscribed "Eliza," a present from her mother Annette Reed de la Renta, rests on a living room table. The small framed landscape is a painting by George Innes.

Below: The bedroom painted the color of a ticket stub from a museum in Europe. The Dutch leather painted screen belonged to Eliza's mother and was photographed in her bedroom by Horst.

Opposite: A view from the living room into the dining room. The large circular dining table, a "jupe" table, mid-18th century, is made up of pie-shaped wedges, removable to make the table smaller. The large English Queen Anne Pier mirror, early-18th century, is a gift from Eliza's mother.

Next page: Emma and Fred in the kitchen waiting for dinner. The prints on the wall are from Robert Thorton's "The Temple of Flora," the first comprehensive botanical survey (19th century).

Last spread: Eliza in the living room. The 19th-century Ziegler rug belonged to Eliza's mother. Above the mantle, a 19th-century Orientalist painting.

"It's a great luxury to be able to have people over to your home for dinner," he continues. "And we try to do it at least once a month. Our table seats ten comfortably, but we have twelve chairs just in case. It's important to me that the dining room feels like the heart of the house."

No matter how casual the dinner party may be, Eliza and Alex have to banish the dogs to the bedroom until the last guest has said goodnight. Eliza couldn't bare another mishap like the one that happened when Fred was only ten weeks old. "Freddy was only a puppy and he just chewed apart a friend's beautiful croc evening bag," explains Eliza.

In 1968, Eliza's mother, Annette Reed de la Renta, one of New York's legendary tastemakers, lived not far from where the Bolens live now. Her apartment was photographed by Horst for *Vogue*, Eliza's great heritage from which to draw inspiration and confidence. Some pieces from that apartment are to be found in the younger couple's home. Eliza and Alex form a perfectly modern counterpoint to that earlier portrait of classic New York grace and style. "Style has a lot to do with the way one's brought up and the environment you grow up in," says Eliza. "At first, my mother's house probably appears very fancy and formal, but it's really very cozy. And I think there are elements of that in the way we live." Alex adds, "I'd say we're serious plagiarists. Do we have a style sense of our own? Sure. But it's more about what we like, what we're used to, and what's comfortable."

What is your idea of earthly happiness?
Health, family, friends.

To what weaknesses are you most indulgent?
Ice cream.

Who are your favorite heroes of fiction?
James Bond.

Who are your favorite heroes in real life?
Educators.

Who are your favorite characters in history?
Winston Churchill.

Who is your favorite painter?
Jan Vermeer.

Who is your favorite musician?
The Beatles.

Who is your favorite writer?
Mark Twain.

What is the quality you most admire in a man?
Integrity.

What is the quality you most admire in a woman?
Compassion.

What is your favorite occupation?
Eliza: Being with my dogs. Alex: Fishing.

Who would you have liked to be?
Leonardo da Vinci.

What is your most marked characteristic?
Trustworthiness.

What is your favorite color?
Eliza: Green. Alex: Red.

What is your favorite bird?
The eagle.

PEGGY AND SEBASTIAN GUINNESS

"It's like an oasis in SoHo," says Peggy Stephaich Guinness of the Manhattan 19th-century loft-cum-*pied-à-terre* she shares with her husband Sebastian and their Cairn terrier, Gypsy. "Everyone who walks in here says it doesn't feel like New York. It feels very Asian." The large-scale, comfortable furniture, much of it garnered in places like Brazil, China, Bali, and Spain, invites lounging. The floors are the original cherry wood. The wooden windows, pleasingly old and full of gaps, sing on windy days.

This is the quintessential Bohemian studio. Objets d'art are deposited here on the way back from one place, on the way to another: from the Far East, Amazon Indian featherhead pieces and masks, Tibetan religious images, Indonesian textiles, and almost lost amongst all this exotica, a little pillow embroidered with the word Foxcroft, the conservative Virginia boarding school where Peggy was educated. "This place is a real combination of our collections," says Sebastian. "I'd say it's pretty Victorian in taste at the moment—full of clutter." "It just came together like this," says Peggy. "We just moved in with all our stuff and found places for it. It couldn't really be called 'decorating.' It just happened."

Sebastian, a direct descendant of Arthur Guinness, who founded Dublin's world-famous Guinness brewery in 1759, is a photographer and documentary filmmaker. Mekong Productions is his baby. He produces his own films and is currently in the middle of a five-year project chronicling Indonesia's transition to democracy. He had spent several years in Tibet on various projects, fulfilling a life-long fascination with the Far East.

Peggy was born in America, but grew up in France. Her maternal grandmother, a Mellon from Pittsburgh, was married to Tommy Hitchcock, the ten-goal polo player who achieved worldwide fame in the 1930s. When she was 19, Peggy went to visit her brother in Sao Paulo, Brazil, and ended up staying for the next eleven years. "I just fell in love with the beauty of the place," she says. "I felt, and still feel, a strong connection to the land, the people, the music, and the art." Turned on by the energy and sensuality of life in Brazil, Peggy began designing jewelry using the distinctive native materials. "I just started playing with it, really," she says. Her favorite stones—tanzanite, citrine, tourmaline—all come from Brazil. Her designs have been featured in all the major fashion magazines and praised for their innovative use of new materials, boldness, and youthful spirit. "They can be easily worn with jeans by day, then to cocktails at night," said one writer.

The couple's New York home couldn't be more different from their main residence, a former monastery on top of a mountain in northern Spain. "We have 70-mile views out to the sea," says Sebastian. "It's a drafty old confection with a large chapel and a pool." Sebastian spends only about three months a year in New York. Peggy stays here a bit more. "It's a good place to find new projects; a great place to edit; and a good place to raise finances when I need to," says Sebastian. "But apart from that, I just love New York and spending time here." "It's the best city in the world right now," says Peggy.

Previous page: Peggy and Sebastian Guinness in their eclectic loft in SoHo. Peggy wears a large red coral necklace she designed.

Above: Sebastian stands in the kitchen in front of an old advertisement for Guinness beer, "Waterloo bridge is coming down. Guinness for strength."

Below: Jewelry designed by Peggy spread about the dining room table.

Opposite: A view of Broadway from one of the many large windows in the loft. On the sill, a photograph of Peggy's grandfather, Tommy Hitchcock, one of the world's greatest polo players, next to Sebastian's Kris collection from Indonesia. Peggy's Hungarian ancestry is shown framed in Stephaich family crest.

Next page: Peggy and Sebastian at the entrance to the living area of the loft. Sebastian wears a purple velvet dinner jacket and trousers made from an Indonesian Ikat.

What do you regard as the lowest depth of misery?
A wet winter in London.

Where would you like to live?
Don't give a monkey's ass as long as it's beautiful.

What is your idea of earthly happiness?
Being at sea.

To what weaknesses are you most indulgent?
Indolence.

Who are your favorite heroes of fiction?
Wily Coyote.

Who are your favorite heroes in real life?
Gus Dor or Abdulrachman Wahid (President of Indonesia).

Who are your favorite characters in history?
Richard Burton.

Who is your favorite painter?
Wyndam Lewis.

Who is your favorite musician?
Valentine from Darling.

Who is your favorite writer?
Robert Graves.

What is the quality you most admire in a man?
Calmness.

What is the quality you most admire in a woman?
Sense of humor.

What is your favorite virtue?
Loyalty.

What is your favorite occupation?
Ranting.

Who would you have liked to be?
Any insurgent.

What is your most marked characteristic?
Disorganized thinking.

What do you most value in your friends?
Ability to suffer in silence.

What is your principle defect?
Rushing around pell-mell.

What to your mind would be the greatest of misfortunes?
Being eaten alive by cannibals, like an oyster. Oh, the pain!

What is your favorite color?
Mediterranean blue, indigo.

What is your favorite bird?
The kingfisher.

AERIN LAUDER AND ERIC ZINTERHOFER

"The way I dress and like to live are always classic," says Aerin Lauder, when asked to describe her personal style. "Instead of trekking to Nepal, I love going to Palm Beach and Long Island. Some people may call that boring; I call it classic."

With her clean, fresh-faced looks and taste for simplicity in dress, Aerin herself is a quintessential all-American woman. She is a real powerhouse at Estée Lauder, the glamour cosmetics label founded by her grandmother, Estée. It is generally assumed that the 30-year-old is being groomed to one day lead the gigantic company, taking over from her uncle Leonard and father Ronald.

Aerin, her husband Eric Zinterhofer, and their baby son, Jack, recently moved into one of Park Avenue's most stately buildings. With the birth of baby Jack, the couple realized they needed more room. Aerin first glimpsed the empty apartment on a snowy day. "I fell in love with its urbane, *Age of Innocence* polish. The casement windows sold me," she recalls. "They looked so elegant and old-fashioned. I could see the snow falling through the old glass. I loved it."

Aerin had collaborated with Jacques Grange, the talented French decorator, on the first apartment she and Eric shared, and loved his sense of proportion and his way with fabrics. She unhesitatingly enlisted him to pull the public rooms of the new apartment together. The library, living room, and dining room all flow *en enfilade* and have been treated by "Jacques" as a unified space. New York decorator Victoria Borus and color specialist Donald Kaufman created more intimate areas in the bedrooms, kitchen, and connecting hallways. The master bedroom is painted powder blue, while the hallway is a soft green. The two colors meet in the kitchen with its blue floor and green walls.

The obvious influence on Aerin Lauder's sense of style was her grandmother, who loved beautiful fabrics and pillows and lived in the luxurious manner of an earlier era. Aerin gives example: "Throughout her houses, Estée always had beautifully-monogrammed matchbooks and bowls of nuts and candy." In a sentimental gesture, for her personal dressing room, Aerin tracked down the same handpainted wallpaper Estée always used.

"I used to love going into my grandmother's bathroom and looking at her vanity," Aerin once told *Vogue*. "She always had the most beautiful make-up tables—in all her houses she would have her antique perfume bottles, her Youth Dew, her favorite make-up. Just tons of lipsticks and eye shadows. Always Estée Lauder, of course." With such a marked affinity for Estée's tastes, it was inevitable that Aerin would go to work for the company that bears her family name.

When Aerin was a teenager, her father Ronald Lauder served as United States Ambassador to Austria for a couple of years and she credits her experiences in Europe for forming her wide-ranging tastes. "We traveled all over the continent and visited the great houses. It really opened my eyes to all sorts of things. That's why my taste is eclectic, not just French, English, or American."

Aerin has begun to recognize other ways in which her style has been influenced by her par

Previous page: Aerin Lauder Zinterhofer in a lilac Tuleh dress stands in the entrance hall with her King Charles Spaniel, Chelsea. A Beauvais tapestry from the first half of the 18th century is on the wall behind her. The 12-branch silver leaf chandelier, French 1930s, is of rock crystal and amethyst beads.

Above: Leopard club chairs in the living room next to a Jean-Michel Frank coffee table. Seen in the distance, Rateau dining room chairs and a Rhulman chandelier.

Below: Leather club chairs by Alfred Porteneuve, circa 1935, in the study. A 16th-century oil-on-oak panel portrait of Pope Jerome by Jan Gossaert (Called Mabuse) above the mantle.

Opposite: Aerin and Chelsea in the living room. Two silver Buccellatti shells are on the Jean-Michel Frank coffee table. The rose-filled vase, antique English glass.

ents. They had always been more interested in 20ᵗʰ-century art and design, and have started to impart some of their appreciation to their oldest daughter. Aerin has developed an eye for French furniture of the 1930s by designers like Jean-Michel Frank, Armand-Albert Rateau, and Jean Royère. Her favorite piece in the apartment is the library's chandelier, which used to hang in fashion designer Jeanne Lanvin's Paris home. Her father actually found it for her and it was the first piece she and Eric bought for their new apartment. The chandelier quickly became the cornerstone from which the rest of the design developed. "All those endless walks down the Rue Bonaparte finally rubbed off," says Aerin.

Though she's assumed a role as a leader of New York's younger social set, Aerin Lauder's no-nonsense approach to life and style is evident in her clothes and home. "I'm just very traditional."

Aerin in her bedroom. In the foreground, a round parchment coffee table with starburst pattern top by Samuel Marx (Chicago, circa 1945).

What is your idea of earthly happiness?
My family—no question.

To what weaknesses are you most indulgent?
White bread.

Who are your favorite heroes of fiction?
The Black Stallion.

Who are your favorite heroes in real life?
Colin Powell.

Who are your favorite characters in history?
Anne Frank, Abraham Lincoln.

Who is your favorite musician?
Madonna.

What is your favorite occupation?
Being a mother.

Who would you have liked to be?
Nursery school teacher.

What is your most marked characteristic?
My laugh, my smile.

What is your principle defect?
Bad eyesight—to which I rarely admit.

What is your favorite color?
Blue.

What is your favorite bird?
Roasted chicken.

Aerin and Eric share a dance.

NICOLAS BERGGRUEN

Perched high above Grand Army Plaza, on the 31st floor of the Pierre Hotel, with spectacular views of Central Park, rests the bachelor pad of Nicolas Berggruen. But if the bachelor pad moniker conjures up images of empty take-out containers and futon furniture, this is another story. Three unique elements make this one sleek apartment: the incredible views, the design by the maestro of minimal chic, architect Peter Marino, and the art, works by many of the most important artists of the second half of the 20th century. The combined effect is stunningly sophisticated.

Nicolas Berggruen is as refined as his apartment. Born in Paris and brought up in France, Switzerland, and England, New York has been his home since 1979. "London may be the current center of Europe," he says, "But New York is always the center of the world." The son of the renowned art collector and dealer Heinz Berggruen, Nicolas went his own way twelve years ago when he and a partner founded his own investment firm, now a monumental success. For Nicolas, his work is his existence—though he has an admirable sense of humor about it. Asked what his favorite object in the apartment is, he replies, "The telephone, and I'm not kidding. It's my life."

But he loves his apartment—the location, the thick old walls, the well-proportioned rooms, the light, the height. "Hotel amenities round the clock are just the icing on the cake." The bold yet simple design that he chose for the apartment works well with his French furniture from the 1930s and 40s, and also, with his extoundingly thorough collection of contemporary art in which Basquiat, Clemente and Kiefer are prominent. His specialty is Andy Warhol, who he feels is the single most important artist in the post-World War II era.

Previous page: Nicolas Berggruen in the living room. A pair of black and white paintings from the Rorschach series by Andy Warhol (1984) hangs above the demi-lune mirror and chrome bronzed consoles. "Big Vase with Veiled Woman" by Picasso sits on the left console. The rectangular mirrored coffee table in the foreground is Sam Marx, the brown pattern and beige chairs are Jean-Michel Frank.
Left: A jardinière sculpture by both Giacometti and Dufy, against Jean-Michel Basquiat's "Tuxedo."
Above: Warhol's Rorschach series seen through the 19th-century Portuguese rosewood four poster bed in Nicolas's bedroom. A silk throw from Thailand is tossed over the chair.
Right: "Drills" (1960) and "Avanti Cars" (1962), both by Warhol, hang above the library desk. The chair is Jean-Michel Frank.
Next page: "Silver Liz" by Warhol in the entrance hall. Warhol's "Last Supper" (1986) hangs on top of a walnut and parchment cabinet by Pierre Chareau.

"He really understood the world we live in. He basically took our daily lives and put them on the wall." Clearly, the collecting gene runs in the family, but Nicolas has no desire to compete with his father. "I was privileged to grow up in an environment where my father collected extensively," he remembers. "I would see a lot of things, and was influenced by them. But it was an informal education, and I was allowed to glean from it just whichever parts appealed to me. My father collects a different generation, and his collection is much larger and goes much deeper. His philosophy is that it is better to stick with one artist than to jump around to many—he concentrates on maybe six artists all together. And I do agree with that. That's why I concentrate on Warhol. It's only significant if you make an effort."

As for his personal style, Nicolas Berggruen likes to be fashionable, elegant—and slightly hard-edged, a quality which is reflected in his choice of art. "There are no 'pretty' pictures in my apartment," he says. "I don't like 'pretty.' Take the Warhol Disaster series. Electric chairs and accidents are not a pleasing subject. But I like things that provoke thought and reaction. I'm opposed to the merely decorative; I prefer things to be visually challenging." Still, with all the hard edges in the rest of the apartment, Nicolas's bedroom was designed to be a quiet and peaceful environment for thinking and sleeping. There are even two enormous stuffed teddy bears on the bed. "Those are 'accidents,' gifts from past girlfriends!" he says, laughing. Now that his bachelor pad visions have been realized, Nicolas dreams of building a place by the water, where he can be alone to think and work. He would love to utilize his passion for art and building by commissioning a great architect to create something terrific. "That would be quite a thrill," he says, with typical restraint and understatement.

SOLEDAD AND ALESSANDRO TWOMBLY

Upon the birth of their second child, and after several years in New York, Soledad and Alessandro Twombly decided to pack up their Gramercy Park apartment and move to Rome. Alessandro, an artist and the son of abstract painter Cy Twombly and portraitist Tatiana Franchetti, was raised in La Dolce Vita-era Rome and his parents still reside in Italy.

Soledad, who travels the world in search of interesting new and antique textiles to use in her line of clothing, was born in Buenos Aires where her father is now mayor. Initially, Alessandro and Soledad were wary about settling in New York and felt it was not the best place to raise a family. They also felt that the daily grind of life there did not benefit their creative spirits. Still, their careers require spending some time in Manhattan.

The solution was this small but personality-filled *pied-à-terre* on lower Fifth Avenue in Greenwich Village. "The very day we decided to move, Alessandro picked up *The New York Times* and declared that he was going out to find an apartment," remembers Soledad. "I thought, 'Good luck.' But he did it. And now we love this building." No wonder: it possesses a crumbling grandeur that would not be out of place in the Italian capital.

Perhaps it reminded them of Cy Twombly's abode in an ancient Roman palazzo, which caused quite a stir in 1966 when *Vogue* published pictures of it. The writer Valentine Lawford called it "serenely pale" and extolled the dramatic effect of its series of grandly-proportioned, white-washed rooms which had been stripped of almost all ornament and color. The pared-down aesthetic and studiedly haphazard placement of sculpture, antique furniture, and Twombly's own massive, thought-provoking canvasses were a revelation to readers. The only flashes of color, the story suggested, came from six-year-old Alessandro, romping around in bright, child-sized versions of 19th-century soldiers' uniforms and wielding a play sword.

Alessandro and Soledad spend about two weeks every three months in New York. Soledad is proud to claim that they decorated their home by themselves. "We are both artists, we don't need a decorator," she says. The first thing they did was paint all the walls white. "Objects show up better against a plain backdrop," she explains. Alessandro, whose strength lies in visualizing where furniture and paintings would look best, organized the space, while Soledad chose all the fabrics. The textiles change constantly, depending on her latest finds and inspirations. Recent trips to India and the Far East produced the curtains and sheets; she's piled brilliantly-colored ikats from Indonesia on a chair just to enjoy the flash of color against the white walls; the sitting room carpet was bought in China; and as for the piece of dark pink antique silk tossed over the sofa today, tomorrow it may be replaced by one of emerald green.

But the real decoration comes from the art. Terra cotta sculpture, animal bones, and other odd finds are displayed on a rough-hewn table. Many of the paintings are by Alessandro himself. As a rule, Alessandro refuses to live among his own canvases and sculptures, but this is their *pied-à-terre*, their home away from home. As might be expected, there are a pair of paintings by Alessandro's father, as well as an Alberto di Fabio, and an Yves Klein that was given to the couple as a wedding present. Antique photographs of Rome and its surrounding aqueducts remind them of their other home.

For travel-weary artists like the Twomblys, this charming retreat is a welcome place to rest their heads. "Home, for me, is a place where I can wake up at 3 in the morning and walk around and look at things and enjoy them. It's wonderful to have a chance to sit uninterrupted and really look at a painting that you haven't seen in a while. I love being back in the city," she concludes. "I stay up enjoying all the noise—the traffic, the sirens. It's funny, but you do start to miss those sounds when you leave New York."

Previous page: Soledad Twombly on a day bed covered with a throw from Gaia Franchetti's textile line, "Indoroman." Behind her is a painting by her husband Alessandro Twombly. On the floor, a Turkish kilim. Opposite: "For Alessandro from Papa," painted by Soledad's father-in-law, Cy Twombly, a gift for his son's 18th birthday.

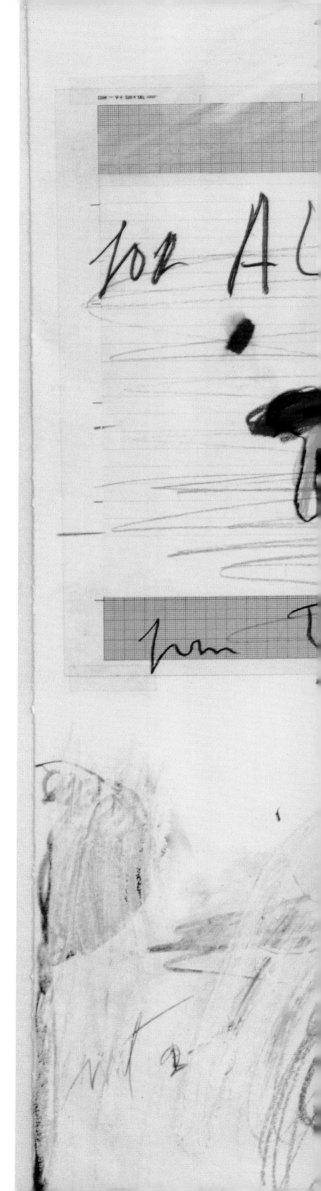

What is your idea of earthly happiness?
Dulce de leche.

To what weaknesses are you most indulgent?
Indecision.

Who are your favorite heroes of fiction?
Sandokan.

Who are your favorite characters in history?
Alexander the Great.

Who is your favorite painter?
Lucio Fontana.

Who is your favorite musician?
Mozart.

Who is your favorite writer?
Jorge Luis Borges.

What is the quality you most admire in a man?
Intelligence.

What is the quality you most admire in a woman?
A sense of humor.

What is your favorite virtue?
Honesty.

What is your favorite occupation?
Sewing.

Who would you have liked to be?
A ballet dancer.

What is your principle defect?
I get bored easily.

What to your mind would be the greatest of misfortunes?
Losing my family; I can't imagine anything worse.

What is your favorite bird?
The cuckoo bird.

Right: A view of the living room's rustic pine table on which rests many of Alessandro Twombly's sculptures, an Impala skull and a large piece of driftwood. The paintings above and below the table are by Alessandro. The two black and white photographs, left, are Roman aqueducts. Soledad found the carpet in Central China.

The greatest style is with the young who do not know they have it. I don't know how to write about style, as it's evanescent. I can say however that style has no age, that it's just style, you either have it or you don't. This is just one more injustice of life.

My husband always gives the following story as an example of great style. He was walking into dinner at Daisy Fellows' (Mrs. Reginald Fellows) in the South of France with a girl he had brought. Mrs. Fellows was standing by the terrace door dressed all in white as Peggy Scott-Duff, his date, accidentally spilled Dubonnet down the front of Daisy's dress. Mrs. Fellows looked down and then looked at a terrified Peggy, smiled and said, "Don't worry darling, white is such a boring color." That is style, to have manners always and with everyone.

CAROLINA HERRERA

Personal style is a secret known only to the person who has it.

BILL BLASS

When I hear the phrase "Bright Young Thing" I think of the good old days, when we girls read Tolstoy and Henry Adams and thought more of our reading than of our dressing. As typical young women, we were dressed neatly and very much the same. The one who started to wear something different was usually laughed about, rather than congratulated for her attempts at the latest fashion.

BROOKE ASTOR

Never define your own style, you might lose it by copying yourself.

ANH DUONG

MICHELLE AND GEORGE ANDREWS

Their passion for art brought George and Michelle Andrews together. In 1991, Michelle was building a serious collection of photography, while George, an actor, was concentrating on paintings. (A mutual friend arranged an introduction.) "She knew that both of us were really involved and engaged with collecting and thought we should meet," says Michelle. "We ended up going to openings and shows together all the time. Pounding the pavement between galleries on Saturdays was central to our courtship." Now, nine years later and with two young sons added to the family, George and Michelle still manage to indulge their love of the arts. They travel to Europe two or three times a year just to see shows and search out new artists and new work. And they never miss the Biennale in Venice. Among their friends are many of the artists. "We concentrate on contemporary art—work made since 1960," says Michelle. "One of the attractions to contemporary art is that you can get to know the artist. It gives you a much deeper appreciation of the work."

In fact, their loft once belonged to friends Julian Schnabel and his first wife, Jacqueline; they raised their two daughters there and then sold the place to another artist, Anselm Kiefer. When George and Michelle married, they realized they needed a place that could hold their combined collections. The duplex loft in Chelsea fit the bill. Before they took possession, the Schnabels walked George and Michelle through their old space, reminiscing about the time they had lived there. They were distraught over the condition it was in as Kiefer had removed all of Schnabel's grand touches. "A sure clash of the titans," says George. "A question of one artist not wanting vestiges of another invading his space."

First page: George and Michelle Andrews at a desk by Charlotte Perriand. Behind them, a Cindy Sherman photograph and a Donald Baechler painting from the Crowd series. The black spider lamp, 1950, was designed by French engineer Serge Mouille. The bookcases are steel, floor to ceiling, and cover entire wall. Previous spread: The living room. "Monument" by Christian Boltanski above a straw marquetry cabinet by Jean Royère. The rug is by Coglin. Above: A corner of the loft's living area. A unique pony skin lucite chaise designed by Tom Ford. On the small table by Frank Lloyd Wright, a one of a kind lamp, a collaboration between Giacometti and Jean-Michel Frank. Below: A suite of furniture makes for a secluded sitting area. The Sam Marx's furniture, from a Chicago estate sale, is in its original configuration. In the background, George and Michelle's bedroom. Opposite: The entrance. A pair of Sam Marx craquelure chests sit back to back. On the wall, the first photographs by Bruce Nauman.
Next page: The bathroom. Cameron and Aidan Andrews play in the marble sarcophagos tub. Above them, a photograph by Ann Hamilton and a sconce by Jouve. The chairs in the foreground are Marc du Plantier.

George and Michelle are indulgent and relaxed parents. No area of the loft is off-limits to their boys Cameron, 4, and Aidan, 18 months. They run happily through the treasures. Most of the family activities take place in the large central room. Michelle loves being aware of what everyone is up to. "I can hear them laughing and playing even when I'm working on my own," she says. In addition to all the art surrounding them, the apartment has front-row seats for some great performances. At first glance, the back windows of the apartment seem only to face the dark backside of another building. But look more closely and you're apt to see tutus and toe shoes; 20 feet across a dark alley, the windows look directly into the dance studios of the American Ballet Theater. For hours on end, the Andrews can watch the ballerinas and dancers perfect their *passés* and *relevés* before they take the stage at Lincoln Center. Dancer/choreographer Mark Morris also rehearses in the space and has since befriended young Cameron, who has become a fan.

After the birth of Aidan, Michelle decided to leave the corporate world, where she'd been a management consultant at McKinsie & Company, and try her hand at something new. These days she refers to herself as an "aesthetic consultant, for lack of a better term." It was an easy transition. Friends were always asking for her help in locating art and furniture and even apartments, so she decided to do it full-time. "I kind of feel like a curator, a lifestyle curator," she says. "Many of my clients are just moving to New York and I can get involved from the very beginning, looking for the actual living space itself. I take a wholistic approach to developing a lifestyle for them in the city. For others, I'm just on the lookout for things that will work with or enhance a collection they've begun." She seems to have an encyclopedic knowledge of 20th-century art and design and collects formidable modern French design. In the living room furniture by such designers as Jean Royère, Jean Prouvé, Marc du Plantier, Charlotte Perriand, and Serge Mouille complement artworks by Cindy Sherman, Donald Baechler, Phillip Taafe, Julian Schnabel, and others. "Everyone, including George, teases me because I'm always moving things around," says Michelle. "One of the things that draws me to objects is that I love placing them and bringing different pieces together to see how they interact. To me, all these objects are art."

PATRICIA HERRERA

Sometimes, the most successful and exciting decorating is often in spots that no one else will ever really see. In the case of Patricia Herrera, a fashion editor at *Vanity Fair*, it makes perfect sense that her little closets received extra attention. Patricia had them upholstered in lush colorful fabrics from floor to ceiling and the effect is like stepping inside a gigantic jewel box. "I don't know the theory behind it," she says, "but I guess it's supposed to be better for the clothes to rest against the fabric than the bare walls or wooden shelves. My mother does it at home."

Patricia is the youngest of the four daughters of fashion designer Carolina Herrera and man-about-town (and *Vanity Fair* Special Projects Editor) Reinaldo Herrera. The family moved to New York from Venezuela when Patricia was nine years old. Patricia inherited aristocratic South American beauty, with black hair and eyes, creamy white skin, and regal bearing. Over the years several photographers have tried to get the shy Patricia to sit for them. The one who probably made the best use of her looks was David Seidner, who modeled his portrait of her on Manet's portrait of a barmaid at the Folies-Bergère. Patricia, dressed head-to-toe in Vivienne Westwood couture, bears an uncanny resemblance to the young woman in the painting.

A glance around Patricia's one-bedroom, garden-level apartment in a townhouse on a Greenwich Village street will confirm that the 26-year-old has inherited her mother's appreciation for fabrics. Several swatches are arranged on the arm of one of the couches as she decides which would make the prettiest pillows. "I am always going to fabric stores on the Lower East Side to look for something. Either for here, or for clothes, or for anything I want to make." Patricia didn't own much furniture before she moved into the apartment last year. And she didn't spend a fortune: white, overstuffed sofas, from Crate and Barrel, lamps Pottery Barn, and the simple table, Macy's trusty furniture department. "I don't have enough money to buy good antiques," says Patricia. "But I'm lucky to have many things that were given to me by my family—a clock that belonged to my grandmother, my grandfather's hatbox. After you have the basic stuff like couches, it's nice to have a hint of history and to carry a little bit of your family around with you wherever you go."

The garden, bigger than the apartment, becomes another room in the summer. "On the weekends, if I'm in town, I love to have friends over for breakfast. The only thing I can cook is breakfast. I'm really good at omelets, but that's about it." She painstakingly arranges little window boxes and other containers and plants bulbs and rosebushes to bloom in the spring. "Last year," she sighs, "I had amazing jasmine trees. They were night blooming, so the garden had the most unbelievable fragrance the next morning. One harsh New York winter was enough to do them in, though. Very upsetting. This year I bought wisteria instead."

Patricia's parents have taken a special interest in her apartment. "My mother has keys and will stop by and leave things all the time," says Patricia. One day, Patricia came home to find that her mother had tackled the self-imposed task of furniture arrangement. "I'll be at work, and I'll get a phone call from my dad. He'll say, 'I'm sitting in your bedroom reading and watching your mother work in the garden.' It's so funny. Their home is really sophisticated and grand, but they love it here. I get jealous and wish I could join them."

Previous page: Patricia Herrera stands among the rhododendron in her garden on Bank Street. She's wearing a pink satin evening gown designed by her mother, Carolina Herrrera.
Opposite: Patricia seen through the bedroom casement windows.
Above. A putti, once in Patricia's bedroom in Venezuela, sits on top of a table from Macy's furniture department. Below: The table shows a framed Polaroid of a photograph taken by Annie Leibovitz for *Vogue*. Patricia poses together with her mother and her sister Carolina.

JANE LAUDER

Jane Lauder's loft-like penthouse apartment practically glows. Sunlight enters from three directions. The bedroom receives the rousing morning sun, while the living room catches the sunset and an unequaled view of the Carlyle Hotel. A clean northern light, so beloved of artists, illuminates all day, any day, works by Matisse, Jasper Johns, Ellsworth Kelly, Warhol, Lichtenstein, de Kooning, and John Chamberlain.

"My father started giving me art when I was younger," she explains. "And recently I've started buying on my own. My parents collect a lot so I've learned from them, and it's great because I can also borrow stuff," Jane says.

The art isn't the only modern element in this apartment. Jane is the 26-year-old granddaughter of Estée Lauder, founder of the luxury cosmetics empire of the same name. Like her sister Aerin and her father and uncle before her, Jane works in the family business. Her style is clean, simple, and all about good design; her abode, ultra-modern, and more than a touch glamorous.

It took a year and a half of work to create the pristine environment. Jane commissioned architects John Keenen and Terry Riley of Keenen/Riley to create a loft space out of what was originally a more traditional layout. Terry Riley is no less than the chief curator of architecture and design at the Museum of Modern Art.

It was a bigger challenge than anyone expected. To achieve the loft feeling, a clean, simple box with zones fluidly connected, the space had to be gutted, rebuilt from scratch. "Once we started doing that, other problems emerged and it got more complicated," says Jane. "It ended up taking so much longer than I ever thought and sometimes it was really frustrating. But it was worth it. I love my apartment so much now. I think John and Terry did an amazing job."

Why didn't Jane just buy an actual Downtown loft? "That's a good question but it's easy to answer. I wanted to be Uptown near my family—they all live within a few blocks of here. And to be honest I just fell in love with this place when I saw it. It's up high and the terrace is amazing. I don't think that lofts Downtown often have that combination."

Floating on an ethereal cloud amidst between-the-wars buildings of New York, Jane's place is full of surprises. Tables and stools by Frank Lloyd Wright and a chair by Alvar Aalto grace the living room. The dining set was designed by Richard Neutra, and in the chandelier's usual place over the table, Jane whimsically hung a Calder mobile. At the touch of a button, a screen lowers from the ceiling in front of the fireplace and black-out shades cover the windows to turn the living room into a private theater. Only the popcorn is missing. "I go out a lot and travel so much for work that I miss all of the great movies. My favorite of all time is *Raiders of the Lost Arc*. Nothing better than curling up and gazing at Harrison Ford for the evening."

Previous page: Jane on her wrap-around terrace swing. Behind, the tower of the Carlyle Hotel.
Left: The front hall designed by architects Terry Riley and John Keenen as a gallery space. Jane stands alongside a Jasper Johns and a wall of Matisse cut-out prints.

Above: The sculpture on the Frank Lloyd Wright desk is by John Chamberlain. The Arco chrome lamp is from the 1960s. To the left, a corner of a Warhol print from the Flowers series, next to a small cushioned side stool by Frank Lloyd Wright.
Below: The living room stool and a pair of small tables are Frank Lloyd Wright. The bronze sculpture is by Jean Arp and the white painting by Ellsworth Kelly.
Opposite: Jane's dining room. A Calder mobile hangs over the table and the chairs are Richard Neutra. The back wall panels open up to the kitchen.

NANCY AND ANDREW JARECKI

Having made her way to New York via the Great Plains of Kansas and Los Angeles, Nancy Jarecki is a breath of fresh air in Gotham's often overheated social hothouse. She definitely likes to do things her own way and nowhere does it show more than in the way she decorated her young family's mock Tudor-style abode in a turn-of-the-century Upper East Side co-op apartment house designed in 1906 by the renowned architect Charles Platt, Jr. To step across the threshold of the apartment is to leave the building's chic hush behind and enter a cozy, active, homey realm. One would probably be offered a glass of lemonade as shown about.

Passionately-collected mementos and artworks crowd walls, shelves and tabletops—but the place never feels cluttered. Nancy, a painter who set her work aside a few years ago to raise her two young sons, Maxson, eight, and Jasper, three, channels the energy she once used in her art into the house and her life. A decade ago, her husband Andrew founded the groundbreaking Moviefone (a.k.a. 777-FILM), which he then sold to AOL. He still runs it as a division of AOL-Time Warner. They found this apartment just a few years go.

To hear her tell it, it took every bit of her artist's vision to be able to imagine this apartment as a home when they first saw it. "Everything was painted a kind of dull, olive green," she recalls with a shudder. "The walls had years' worth of soot on them. The floors were covered with linoleum and carpet." But Nancy hoped that a treasure laid under the decades of grime and neglect and couldn't help but be wowed by the two-story baronial hall with huge windows, giant fireplace, and balcony overlooking the space from the second story. She decided to forge ahead.

Previous page: Nancy and Andrew Jarecki in the living room as seen from the wooden balcony above. "Honeychild," a painting by Erica Ranee over the mantle lined with dried hydrangeas.
Above: A job well done?
Below: Maxson Jarecki sits cross-legged on top of his bedroom chest. Behind him, a mural of battling dinosaurs and frogs painted by Amit Trainin. Maxson helped sketch the cartoons from his imagination and paint them on the wall.
Opposite: A wall in the study with framed cartoon drawings by John Rosen.
Next spread: Jasper Jarecki with Nancy and Andrew in the living room. The chair is upholstered in pieces of Dalmatic priest's silk garment (French, 1825).

"It was a mess, but I looked at it and I could just see how it would work," Nancy recalls. "And I loved how this room was going to be unusual and dramatic." Still, her battles were far from over. No less than seven contractors advised her to fully gut the place and start from scratch. When Dermot Robinson, her "guru painter," arrived on the scene, he shared her enthusiasm and patience. He walked all over and scratched each surface with a coin. The woodwork he uncovered was more beautiful than anyone had guessed. "Everything—everything—was painted that green," says Nancy, "even some of the floors. But Dermot knew that we'd find wonderful things under that paint. He was a godsend. Everyone laughed at me but him."

It took a year of restoration work before the family could move in. The decor was inspired by an old book on Gilded Age interiors that Nancy found at a flea market. A growing collection of 19th-century Hunsinger chairs flank sofas that she designed herself. Despite the antiques throughout, the home has none of that look-but-don't-touch feel, a danger she made sure to avoid. "You have to be careful that your home doesn't end up looking like a furniture showroom."

To help give the place a more informal feel, Nancy and Andrew enlisted the aid of interior decorator Muriel Brandolini, whose signature is the sumptuous, colorful textiles she finds all over the world. It's an interesting melding of styles. The Civil War-era formal parlor chairs were restored to their natural state, then covered in materials and colors that their original owners could never have imagined. While the great room was made for entertaining (the massive table can seat 22, in grand Henry VIII style), the rest of the more moderately dimensioned rooms are perfect for the family to hang out and relax in. Overall, the home reflects the Jareckis' unconventional approach to life in New York's upper reaches—casual, colorful, and, above all, fun.

DAMIAN LOEB

"Whenever I get a break from painting, I work on fixing up my home and studio, trying to make it my ideal space," says the artist Damian Loeb, whose paintings have been described as Norman Rockwell meets David Lynch. "I am constantly painting or constructing something in the studio, but I've come to accept that I am more interested in the act of working on the apartment than in actually finishing it." Damian has been meaning to sand the rough, unfinished wood floor for months—walking barefoot here is not recommended.

The place has the feel of a wonderful work in progress. It's a live/work situation: a street-level, storefront space in TriBeCa. Two big plate-glass windows flank a set of double doors. Inside are two floors and a sleeping loft Damian built himself. Damian tried to restore as much of the original open store space as possible, while keeping new elements like the sleeping loft as straight, simple, angular, and non-distracting as possible. Since each of Damian's neo-photo-realistic paintings take a month of intense concentration to complete, keeping distractions to a minimum is of premium importance. Even so, the space is not sterile. It's a warm buzzing artist's studio.

Damian Loeb doesn't even try to escape work at the end of the day. "I've never been able to separate the two states of being, so I've resigned myself to living in my studio, versus working in my apartment. When I need to escape, I just turn off the lights so I can't see the mess I've made that day." In any case, since the space is at street-level, he can easily make a quick run for freedom.

It's on those streets that Damian finds most of his inspiration. The fashion that one sees all over New York is something that definitely intrigues him, and that finds its way into his work in all sorts of unusual ways. Fashion designer Alexander McQueen, the head of the French house of Givenchy and a great friend of Damian's, once left his Burberry scarf behind after a visit. Soon enough that distinctive plaid, now a resurrected status symbol on the streets of New York, London, and Paris, found its way onto Damian's next canvas. Art critics have seized on this use of fashion symbols as evidence of superficiality in Damian's work. But the artist is up-front about his interest. "I'm a terribly insecure person," he confides willingly. "I will do whatever it takes to hide my flaws and augment my appearance, and I am fortunate to know people who specialize in catering to people with my particular character flaws. I just follow whatever interests me. That and anything which might make me more desirable as a mate."

Damian Loeb is entirely self-taught. He dropped out of high school in Connecticut and moved to New York fourteen years ago to pursue his dream of being an artist. That streak of independence remains with him to this day. Although he's not a fixture on the New York art scene, with its cocktail parties and gallery openings, and he craves privacy and the time and space to do his own work, Damian's distinctive work has nonetheless found an appreciative and hungry audience. His last two shows at the Mary Boone gallery were sold out before they even opened.

Damian in his artist's studio makeshift living room. Behind him, a small unfinished painting hangs below a primed canvas.

Previous page: Stinky and Fatty, formerly orphaned cats, on the rough wood floorboards. Above: Damian peering out his front door onto Lespinard Street where he finds much of his inspiration. Below, left: "That's my painting ashtray. It's at the perfect height when I'm standing and painting."
Below, right: Detail of Damian's paintbrushes stored in paint cans, separated by different bristle types.
Opposite: Damian's homemade security system. All the parts come from a security and alarm store on Canal Street. The screen shows Damian on the street outside his front door. Last page: Stinky stares out the custom-made "cat window," sanded Plexiglas to let light through at eye-level.

It's hard to say what a glance around the apartment would teach one about Damian, except that he works. He doesn't have much art work, either his own or others', about. The most important object, he claims, is his stereo; the oldest, his teddy bear. ("I've kept him because he's never critical and always discreet.") Damian lives alone. "Well, I seem to be subletting the space from two particularly neurotic cats. I just desperately need to have a place where I can relax and not panic," he says. "I need comfort, protection, privacy, and a place to scream."

What do you regard as the lowest depth of misery?
Self-awareness.

Where would you like to live?
Right where I am, although a castle in Scotland would be nice.

What is your idea of earthly happiness?
Finding and fulfilling my purpose for living; good bagels.

Who are your favorite heroes of fiction?
Don Quixote, Captain Ahab, Howard Roarke.

Who are your favorite heroes in real life?
Travis Bickle, T.S. Garp, Joe Buck, Ratso Rizzo, Benjamin Braddock, Humbert Humbert.

Who are your favorite characters in history?
Caligula, Marquis de Sade, Puck.

Who is your favorite painter?
Jan Vermeer or Bob Ross. Which one painted "Happy Trees"?

Who is your favorite musician?
Richard M. Hall—when I don't owe him any money, that is.

Who is your favorite writer?
William Shakespeare.

What is the quality you most admire in a man?
Dependence, devotion, obedience, and coming when they are called.

What is the quality you most admire in a woman?
Self-sufficiency, aloofness and the ability to purr.

To what weaknesses are you most indulgent?
Lust, greed, sloth, pride, gluttony, envy and wrath, all of which seem to surface in me when I'm around members of the opposite sex.

What is your favorite occupation?
Artist ... no; actor ... no; rock star ... Which one is it everybody loves, again?

What is your most marked characteristic?
Random perfectionism.

What do you most value in your friends?
Their honesty, consistency, or maybe their shortcomings.

What is your principle defect?
My inability to say no, my fear of giving or getting rejected, a propensity for hyperbole, fear of commitment, and, and, and ...

What to your mind would be the greatest of misfortunes?
To die before I figure out what love is; or, that penis-in-the-zipper thing.

What is your favorite color?
Blue. It sells more paintings.

What is your favorite bird?
That one with two fingers on one side and one and a thumb on the other.

MARINA RUST AND IAN CONNOR

One expects the great-great-granddaughter of Marshall Field, founder of Chicago's grandest department store, to have a house full of heirlooms and antiques. Marina Rust's apartment delivers. It fairly creaks at the seams with glamorous family snapshots, her grandfather's books, her grandmother's objets vertus from around the world, and paintings from her father's collection. But Marina, a novelist and contributing editor at *Vogue*, doesn't live in the past. Mixed in with the heirlooms are her own auction and flea market finds. Originally, what drew her to this apartment were the high ceilings. "When I was apartment hunting, my father's first question was always, 'What's the wall space like?' It's always about hanging space for him."

Today, Marina is grateful for her father's insistence on adequate hanging space, and she has certainly inherited his eye (he was the curator of French art at the National Gallery in Washington), for her walls are filled with paintings and drawings by Sargent, Fuseli, and Tchelichew from his collection. In fact she may indeed have the smallest apartment in New York boasting two Sargents.

Once upon a time, with her contrasting dark hair and porcelain skin, Marina Rust herself would have made a perfect subject for a Sargent portrait, yet her accomplishments extend far beyond looks. Her debut novel, *Gatherings*, published in 1993, brought her to the attention of *Vogue* Editor-in-Chief Anna Wintour, who commissioned a story about the young blue-blooded beauty. Shortly after, *Vogue* caught on to Marina's own writing talent and began assigning her regular stories. For two years, in the column "She's Gotta Have It," Marina entertained readers with tales of her quest for that month's fashion must-have, from the perfect pair of sunglasses to just the right shoe. Marina is at work on her second novel and writes for *Vogue*.

Marina's first grown-up decorating experience in New York was a 400-square-foot bijou on East 70th Street. To pull the apartment together, Marina enlisted the aid of the late Mark Hampton, who had decorated her father's house, including Marina's childhood bedroom, in Washington, D.C. Inspired by her aunt Diana Phipps' book *Affordable Splendor: An Ingenious Guide to Decorating Elegantly, Inexpensively, and Doing Most of It Yourself*, Marina painted the bedroom dark blue and covered the living room walls in green-and-white striped fabric gathered into a tent-like canopy on the ceiling. "Fabric-covered walls are a pain," Marina remembers. "They held smells—from cooking or smoking, and now and then there would be a leak from the apartment above that would stain the material."

There's nothing quite so dramatic in her current home though, Marina and Mark Hampton collaborated to create a comfortable, livable space. New furniture like an English colonial reproduction day bed sits alongside family heirlooms and authentic 18th-century English pieces found at auctions. The walls are painted a neutral beige borrowed from the creamy undersides of the large seashells Marina collects. They provide a perfect backdrop for the paintings she has "on permanent loan" from her father.

One might assume that Marina lives alone, as it is her cherished objects that fill the space. But look closely and you'll see signs of her debonair husband, Ian Connor. They were married in the fall of 1999. "Ian didn't bring much," says Marina. "A few items from his childhood and family photographs." Still, Marina claims that her favorite item in the apartment is the gleaming stainless steel Dualit toaster he bought for the kitchen. "I knew the romance would last when he decided he wanted to have breakfast here regularly," she says, laughing. The couple's wedding, held at her great-great-grandmother's house on an island in Maine, was covered extensively by *Vogue*. A hint of the possible influence Ian may exert upon their future life together might be garnered from the fact that he insisted, in recognition of his mother's Norwegian upbringing, that the ceremony be formal. At first, the other summer people were disgruntled by the white-tie mandate on the invitation, but all eventually agreed it cast a most romantic spell—an idyllic start to a union of two traditionalists.

When asked to describe her own style, Marina uses the word "disheveled." While that might be going a bit too far, she does prefer to spend her days in khakis and crisp white shirts (although her collection of exquisite, vintage ball gowns might betray a secret love of good, old-fashioned glamour). This uniform is perfectly suited to the life of a writer. Each day, Marina retreats to a tiny study in the back of the apartment. "I really don't leave the house. If you're a writer, you have to be a homebody. Otherwise you'd be a foreign correspondent or something, tripping around to Tehran or wherever. I'm really happier being home than anywhere else."

Previous page: Marina and her husband Ian Connor on their way home from the Edwardian Ball at the Frick Museum.
Left: Marina poses for *Vogue* on the steps of the Frick Museum with Lauren Dupont and Aerin Lauder.

Previous spread: Family photographs, books and little treasures, in the living room bookcase.
Above, left: A portrait of Marina's father by Walter Stuempfig, Paris, 1956. Above, right: Marina's desk.
Opposite: Marina on a day bed in her living room. Above her, a John Singer Sargent watercolor of a reclining woman next to an ink study of horses
by Eugène Delacroix and pen and wash drawing attributed to Guvarra. The raccoon blanket was a Christmas present from Marina's mother to her father.

What do you regard as the lowest depth of misery?
Haven't been there yet.

What is your idea of earthly happiness?
Dinner with Ian.

To what weaknesses are you most indulgent?
Of my own? Laziness.

Who are your favorite heroes of fiction?
Charlotte from *Charlotte's Web.*

Who is your favorite painter?
Edward Burne-Jones.

Who is your favorite musician?
Bruce Springsteen.

Who is your favorite writer?
Just one? Evelyn Waugh, Joan Didion,
Annie Dillard, E.B. White.

What is the quality you most admire in a man?
Virtue.

What is the quality you most admire in a woman?
Irony.

What is your favorite occupation?
Writing interspersed with cooking.

What is your most marked characteristic?
Bad posture.

What do you most value in your friends?
Discretion.

What is your principle defect?
Sloth.

What is your favorite color?
Apple green.

ALEXANDRA AND ALEXANDRE VON FURSTENBERG

In the early 1990s, a trio of sisters—Pia, Marie-Chantal, and Alexandra Miller—emerged from their sheltered upbringing and took the New York social scene by storm. With a glamorous international background, the daughters of Chantal and Robert Miller (of Duty Free Shops fortune) were a dream come true for bored magazine editors on the lookout for a new, younger crowd to fill their pages. Everyone began to breathlessly chronicle the choices these young women made, from clothing and nightclubs to husbands. The saga reached a pinnacle in the summer of 1995, when Marie-Chantal and Alexandra were married in two of the grandest weddings Society had witnessed in a generation. The sisters have retreated from the public eye since then, preferring to build their own families and careers in the world.

Alexandra, the youngest, married her childhood sweetheart Alexandre von Furstenberg, son of fashion designer Diane and Prince Egon, of the noble Austrian-Italian family. When they moved to Los Angeles soon after, Alexandra, who had studied costume design at Brown University, became a buyer for a small boutique. A few years later the couple returned to New York, and she went to work with her mother-in-law. As Creative Director for Diane von Furstenberg Designs, her job was to breathe new life into the company that had made its name with the ubiquitous wrap dress of the 1970s. She is anything but lost in fashion past, however. A fan of the latest, cutting-edge styles, Alexandra von Furstenberg would never be caught dead in vintage clothing. "I can't stand wearing someone else's old clothes," she says, adding with a laugh, "I had a hard enough time sharing clothes with my sisters."

The place Alexandra and Alexandre now live, on the 22nd floor of a modern Manhattan high-rise, which has been in the Miller family for 15 years, has been home to each of the girls in turn. Alexandra and Marie-Chantal first shared it during their last two years of high school. Pia and Christopher Getty called it home for a while when they were first married. Marie-Chantal and her husband, Prince Pavlos of Greece, followed suit a few years later. Alex and Alex moved in a year ago, before their daughter, Talita, was born. "This place has definitely seen a lot of makeovers in its time," quips Alexandra, who has turned it into her own very personal Zen-inspired retreat.

A white monochromatic palette dominates the home. Much of the furniture is Ralph Lauren. Alongside works by Andy Warhol, Ross Bleckner, and photographer Peter Beard, are black-and-white photos of Alexandra with her sisters and husband taken by various photographers over the years.

Silver and nickel objets d'art accent the rooms. One black lacquered table is covered with about forty silver-dipped shells, most of them Buccellati. Carefully placed around the apartment are the silver boxes which the couple received as wedding gifts, all bearing the von Furstenberg family crest. Even with all these shimmering objets, however, the apartment's most defining feature is ultra-cleanliness. It is pristine. Shoes must be removed at the door; nothing is out of place. In fact, when asked what a

Previous page: Alex and Alex in front of Diane von Furstenberg's studio in West Chelsea.
Top: Alexandra and Talita in the pink nursery. A giant green stuffed frog keeps Talita company. Above: Alexandra peers into the living room. The two zebra stools are Ralph Lauren. A photograph by Peter Beard is above the sofa. Opposite: Alexandra reclining in her sleek, white living room. Behind her, a floor-to-ceiling contemporary mirror framed in carved ebony. A Peter Beard photograph of an African woman and a bronze nude are displayed on the chrome and glass Ralph Lauren console.
Next page: A slip-covered chair with the von Furstenberg crest pulls up to a chrome and cherry wood Ralph Lauren architect's desk in the bedroom.

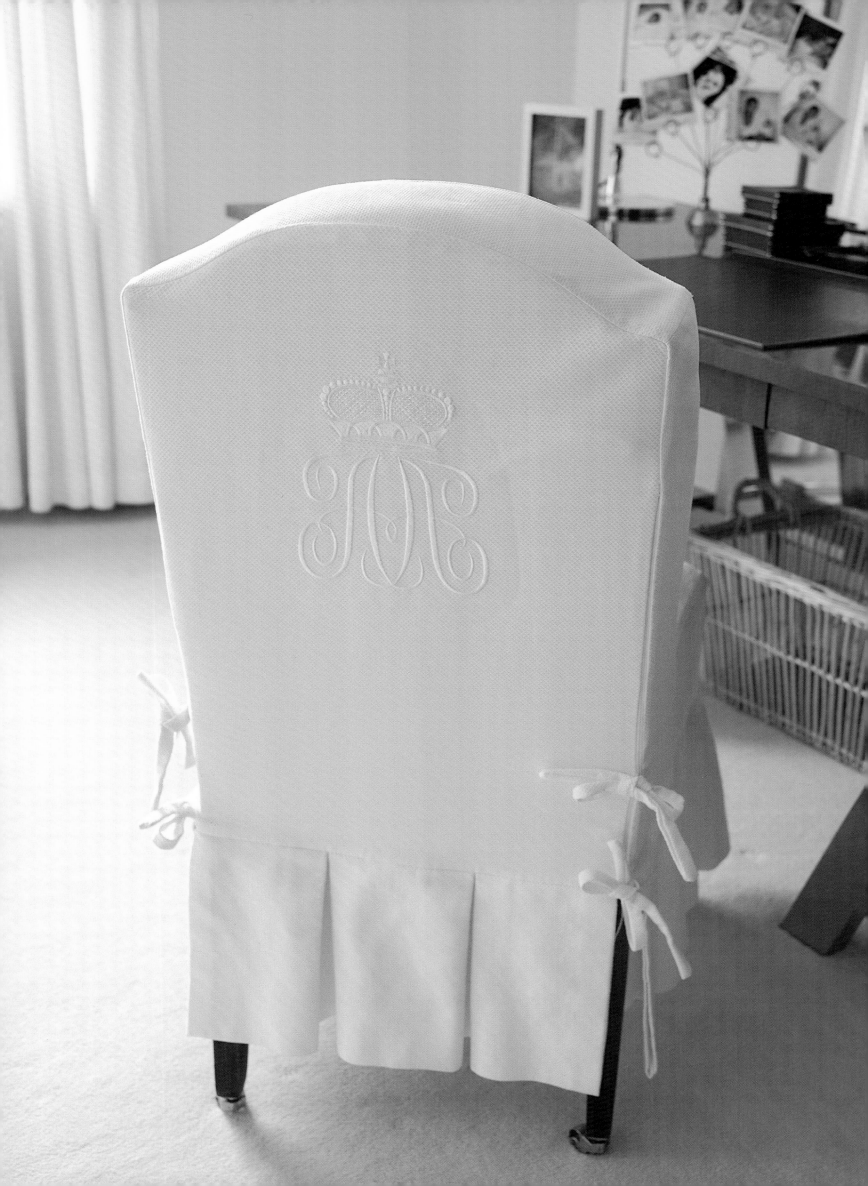

stranger might learn about her from the apartment, Alexandra responds without a moment's hesitation "that I am very clean!"

Their last three homes have been dressed in the same fashion. Alexandra has always been drawn to the spare and minimal look. The Malibu beach house of their friend Sandy Gallin, a Hollywood manager, was a great inspiration. "We just adored it," she says. "The windows were always open and a fresh beach breeze would be blowing in. It was very white. The floors were stained dark—very dramatic. But it was filled with comfortable, big, white furniture with plush pillows. It was such an airy, pleasant space. I really admired that and we've made a New York version that works for us."

Alexandra remembers growing up surrounded by fabrics and heavy textures—"Very Mongardino," she says, referring to the late decorator known for elaborate schemes and dramatic gestures.

"When I went out on my own, I wanted to take a different route. Everything I have in my house is there for a reason," she says. "It is meant to be used in some way, and I don't have too many of any one thing. It's so clean and sparse and white. It's my sanctuary."

So, how does having a baby affect the sense of order and repose that Alexandra von Furstenberg has prepared so well? "Not much," she says. "I never wanted to get too far into babyland. When my daughter was born, I got a small tattoo, a little heart, because I wanted to mark her on me and to mark the occasion. It was something I'd always wanted to do, but never felt like I was able to. But it seemed like once I became a mother myself, no one could tell me not to. So I did it."

Where are the "swans" of yesteryear? Mona Williams, Gloria Guinness, Jacqueline de Ribes, "Slim" Keith, Babe Paley, Jackie Onassis? Only C.Z. Guest remains in New York, wearing her vintage Mainbochers. When fashion comes back to life, let's hope there are fashion "swans" to keep it alive.

ELEANOR LAMBERT

People are always talking about who will be the new Brooke Astor, the new Queen of Society. With all due respect to Mrs. Astor, I think what New York Society really needs is a new Diana Vreeland, someone who knows that in matters of style and social life originality is as important as propriety, as essential as taste, openness as desirable as exclusivity. Perhaps she—or he; a king!— dwells in these pages, ready to burst forth in a new millennial blaze of brilliance, fun and glamour. Pizazz, DV called it.

BOB COLACELLO

The most important thing when you talk about personal
style is knowing that the most aging word is "no" and
that the youngest is "yes." I think it is so important to
say "yes." To have curiosity, energy, to want to know
everything, to be a Bright Young Thing. There is nothing
more than aging to be idle …

OSCAR DE LA RENTA

Express yourself through your rooms. The key words
are verve and nerve.

MARIAN McEVOY

You see it? Then you don't? Style, in today's quick-
access world is mostly invisible, intangible, inarticulate.
You have to dig, almost in archaeologist mode, to
unearth that certain something, that emotion, that icon,
that thing called style.
It is as perfect as fresh egg, plucked from the nest in a
country barn. And there is nothing as stylish as a fresh
egg, in a cup, served up with a great style in beautiful
settings: a window framed with the view of a winter's
blanket of whit, or a verdant green horizon in spring.
Style is phrasing, as in the complexity of Marcel Proust;
as in the easy mother wit, street smarts of a
Fran Lebowitz sentence, as in the invented language of
the great author Toni Morrison.

ANDRE LEON TALLEY

MOBY

For Moby, professionally nomadic, a groundbreaking electronic musician, home is usually a hotel in whatever city he's passing through. "Rarely do I stay in one place for more than about 18 hours," he says. "In fact, it feels strange to be in the same place for two days in a row." Last year's itinerary rambled through 176 cities over four continents. "All I need, and I'm sorry to sound like such an awful 21st-century cliché, is a good phone line and my laptop, although a nice view, good linen, and a kitchen can help a lot, too."

Home base, when he can get to it, is a spare 1,200-square-foot loft space off East Houston Street on New York's hip Lower East Side. It's a light-filled respite for happy returns after extended globe-trotting. The apartment's best features are its airy volume—the ceilings range from 12 to 25 feet high—and the skylights that infuse the space with a soft glow.

The walls are bare but for one painting by his best friend, artist Damian Loeb. "I don't like stuff. My apartment doesn't need more stuff," he states bluntly. He takes great pride in buying little that is unnecessary. Everything in the apartment—from the Saarinen side table to the Danish modern sofa to a genuine fire engine ladder—were simply found on the streets of his neighborhood.

Overall, the aesthetic feels serenely Japanese. "A friend once described it as Zen-Scandinavian with a little early-20th-century modernism thrown in," says Moby. "This apartment likes being clean and it likes being uncluttered, so I function as the immune system, keeping it clean and happy. For many years, I lived in a single room apartment where my work life and my domestic life were sort of indistinguishable. And it drove me crazy. When I was trying to have an honest-to-goodness home life, my music equipment would be sitting there blinking at me. When I was trying to work, my sofa and bed would be calling to me in soft and dulcet tones." The first priority, then, was to create a work area that was completely isolated from the domestic area. At one end, Moby constructed a recording studio. Its walls and ceilings are double thick. Eighteen inches of sand lie beneath the false floor to absorb the sound waves from thumping bass speakers. The neighbors never need hear anything. "I have a fantasy," he confides, "of getting married and moving my studio elsewhere and then turning my current studio into the quietest bedroom in New York."

In this trendiest of neighborhoods, Moby, in his simple bohemian disguise of jeans and sneakers, might have gotten lost in the shuffle. But even the larger-than-life trendsetters of the Lower East Side are outscaled by a gargantuan billboard of Moby, the size of a warehouse building wall. "It's particularly interesting, as the Calvin Klein billboard is only three blocks from my apartment. Seeing as there have been few people in the course of human history who've been represented at 40 feet tall in full color, I consider myself to be part of a very strange group of humans. And I think that I look much nicer on the billboard than I do in real life, so I hope people can hold that image in mind when they meet me and disregard the much less impressive figure that I cut in person."

Calvin Klein Jeans
Dirty Denim

Amoco

He is the first to admit that he's not a serious follower of fashion, but his thoughtful and well-edited approach to living could be a model for us all. "My own personal style is slovenliness to the extreme, which is kind of ironic seeing as how my apartment is so clean. I don't really pay attention to my own appearance. I tend to put on the clothes that I took off the night before (which, not surprisingly, tend to be the clothes that I'd taken off the day before that). But I do care about interior design—almost too much. I can't say what's good or bad, but I can say what appeals to me, and it's a wide range. Design that's beautiful or fascinating or calming or sublime or playful or glorious, it all can appeal to me. I'm not a design fascist—except perhaps in my own head. But I keep it to myself. No one wants to be friends with a design fascist, don't you think?"

First page: Richard Melville, nicknamed Moby, is a distant relative of Herman Melville. Moby hangs upside down in his living room from an old wooden fire engine ladder he found down the street. Previous page: Moby featured in a Calvin Klein billboard on the corner of Broadway and Houston. Left: Moby's bookcase filled with "lots of quasi-pretentious grad-student books and lots of big books about buildings because they seem highbrow." Above the bookcase is an early painting by Moby's best friend Damian Loeb, who repaid one of the many loans Moby had given him while Damian was trying to stay afloat. Below, left: Moby at his kitchen counter. Below, right: Damian Loeb relaxes on the Danish modern sofa. The living room chairs were made in Norway in 1963. Moby found them at Las Venus on Ludlow Street. Opposite: Moby in his studio. Next spread: Moby in his sun-filled living room. He found the two Swedish chairs in the foreground at the flea market. Last page: Moby's itinerary on his keyboard rests on top of a cartoon by Damian Loeb.

What do you regard as the lowest depth of misery?
Debilitating anxiety attacks coupled with the flu.

Where would you like to live?
More places than I could count. The Scottish
Highlands, northern Arizona, the northern island
of New Zealand, Patagonia, Mauritania, etc.

To what weaknesses are you most indulgent?
Adolescent self-pity.

Who are your favorite heroes of fiction?
Prince Mshkin, Lancelot.

Who are your favorite heroes in real life?
Christ, John Cage, Homer Simpson.

Who is your favorite painter?
Marcel Duchamp.

Who is your favorite musician?
George Gershwin.

What is the quality you most admire in a man?
Not taking oneself too seriously.

What is the quality you most admire in a woman?
Intelligence.

Who would you have liked to be?
The man who discovered the secret to immortality
and interstellar space travel.

What is your most marked characteristic?
Baldness.

What do you most value in your friends?
Comfort.

What is your principle defect?
In-breeding.

What to your mind would be the greatest of misfortunes?
To be buried alive.

VALESCA AND MATHIAS GUERRAND-HERMES

The 1999 wedding of New York beauty Valesca Dost to Mathias Guerrand-Hermès, scion of the French fashion house known for its ties, saddles, luggage, and the famous Kelly bag, was quite a celebration. After the ceremony, the 450 guests were whisked off to Marrakesh, home of the groom's family retreat, Ain Kassimou, the former Barbara Hutton estate. Four days of parties and toasting followed the love birds.

Valesca went to school in the United States, but grew up in Canada as a passionate equestrian. It comes as no surprise that the Hermès look is a natural fit for her. Currently, much of her time is spent with the couple's five-month-old son, Lucien, but she still manages to run her own public relations firm for fashion houses and beauty companies.

As most of Mathias's family is involved with Hermès, he felt the need for some distance and the desire to do his own thing. During a brief spell in Buenos Aires working for an investment firm, Mathias, a three-goal polo player, helped the French polo team achieve full glory. So much time on a polo pony made him the most logical advisor to his father and the Hermès artisans, their quest being to perfect the new Hermès polo saddle using, no doubt, the incomparable Argentine leather. In 1996, he returned to the United States to start his own hedge fund, Blue Growth.

Valesca and Mathias are charmed with their New York life. Mathias finds the energy level exhilarating when compared to France, "where things just don't move quite quickly enough." Their apartment is in the luxurious Hôtel des Artistes, just off Central Park, one of the architectural gems of New York's Upper West Side. The nine muses decorate its façade. Inside, resi

Previous page: A view from the carved mahogany staircase of Valesca and Mathias Guerrand-Hermès's apartment.
Above: Valesca on the staircase landing. Above her hangs a small portrait, found at an antique shop in Connecticut, of a monk enjoying his supper of oysters and a glass of wine.
Below: Jean-Michel Folon painted all the programs and menus for Valesca and Mathias's whirlwind of a wedding.
Opposite: Valesca, Mathias and Lucien take their yellow lab Petrouse for a walk on the bridal path in Central Park.

dents have access to a squash court and a grand old swimming pool. Room service comes from the famous Café des Artistes in the building.

The living room is dominated by a dramatic, double-height wall of windows facing the carved mahogany staircase and balcony. The ceiling is hand-painted burgundy and gold Middle Eastern motifs. The apartment suited Mathias's "Hermès" taste to a T. "The Hermès look has always been a part of my life," he explains. "When I was growing up in France, we had no school on Wednesdays, and my father would take me to the Hermès atelier to see all the bags, saddles, luggage, and boots being made. I watched the colors for the silks being chosen, and I became friends with all of the artisans. Today, I wear only Hermès ties and shoes, without question. But occasionally, just occasionally," he says on the sly, "I'll order a suit from an English tailor."

Two folding leather campaign chairs stand ready to be packed and folded for safari or perhaps just a picnic in Central Park. The sleek wooden coffee table with the leather base, the cigar box, and various picture frames, vases, and trays are also Hermès. Hints of a life in Morocco, silks and rugs, give the apartment some exotica which contrasts pleasingly with its Occidental side. Both Mathias and Valesca are fond of contemporary art, especially that of French artist Philippe Pasqua, which fills the entrance way.

As much as they enjoy the apartment, however, they have recently learned to keep its worldly pleasures in perspective: Mathias suffered a near-fatal injury while playing polo last summer, and the accident and recovery process caused him to reassess his life. "I am trying to take things as they come," he says. "For now, I just want to enjoy my wife and my son. I feel more easily pleased than before and I am very excited and happy when I wake up in the morning."

What do you regard as the lowest depth of misery?
Staying in New York over the weekend.

Where would you like to live?
Valesca: Italy. Mathias: Argentina.

What is your idea of earthly happiness?
Mathias: Ten (maybe only five) kids with my wife Valesca in a campo in Argentina.

To what weaknesses are you most indulgent?
Valesca: Extending our vacation by three days.
Mathias: Coming home three days early from vacation to go back to work.

Who are your favorite heroes in real life?
Valesca: My husband and my son.
Mathias: My wife and my son.

Who is your favorite writer?
Mathias: Stendhal and Blaise Cendrars.
Valesca: Albert Camus and Victor Hugo.

Who is your favorite painter?
Beatrice Caracciolo.

What is the quality you most admire in a man?
Mathias: The fact that we always try to please our wives.

What is the quality you most admire in a woman?
Mathias: The fact that they are in charge of everything, while pretending the contrary.

What is your favorite virtue?
Valesca: Loyalty. Mathias: Generosity.

What is your favorite occupation?
Being in love and being parents.

Who would you have liked to be?
Lucien, our son.

What do you most value in your friends?
Valesca: Loyalty. Mathias: They sometimes like me.

Valesca on the balcony. The original pattern ceiling painted in a Middle Eastern palette of burgundy, blue and gold. Valesca and Mathias found the Moroccan lantern in the souk.

MIRANDA BROOKS

"With every plant, you must look at it and say 'you are beautiful' before you stick it in the ground," explains Miranda Brooks, a stunning young landscape designer. That, she claims, is her personal secret to harnessing and creating positive energy when planting a garden. The Miranda Brooks Landscape Design shingle is five years old. Planting gardens and designing outdoor spaces for private clients in France, England, and Turkey, as well as the United States, leave Miranda no time for play. Her first commercial project is the Shore Club Hotel in South Beach, where she and British architect David Chipperfield are creating one unified complex out of what was originally two adjacent pieces of property. "This is very different from what I usually do," she says. "Not only do I have to make it look fabulous, but then I have to figure out how the hell I'm going to fit 375 lounge chairs out there."

Born in Lancashire, England and raised in Hartfordshire, Miranda was indoctrinated into the traditions of English gardening from an early age. When she started her own firm, she had been working for *Vogue* in New York (she is still a contributing editor) and designing gardens for friends on the side. Indulging in a lifelong fascinating with the Moorish gardens of southern Spain, Miranda went straight to India, the birthplace of this gardening style, and spent months touring the Mogul gardens. "Islamic gardens work in hot climates and are good for small spaces, like walled courtyards," she explains. "Originally, the Koran dictated how these gardens were to be laid out and which plants and trees they could contain. But as they moved further afield, to Morocco and Spain, the rules relaxed a bit. The versions found in Spain are true little oases. They are contemplative, sensual spaces." Miranda composes her gardens along similar guidelines, using running water, simple plant material, fruit trees, and beautifully-detailed paving tiles to indulge as many of the senses as possible. Surveying her home, the lower floor of a townhouse in West SoHo, Miranda says, "I've never really concentrated on inside spaces. I do appreciate their beauty, but it's all about outside for me." Hard to believe—Miranda's eclectic good taste is evident everywhere indoors: a cowhide rug on the floor, a large brass chandelier, bowls from India, photographs by her friend Adam Fuss, and two canaries, Jeanne and Gabriel, who share a wooden cage from Spain. "In case you were wondering, my canaries are named after archangels," she says. "My last one, Ariel, was sat on by the cat and is buried outside in the garden." Most of the furniture in the apartment was picked up at the flea market and two large windows are draped with fresh white curtains printed with red poppies. "I adore poppies," says Miranda. "I love irises and peonies, too, but I just love the smell of jasmine."

Miranda's professional side is evidenced by the neatly arranged stacks of files and cabinets, temporarily residing on every spare space in her apartment, before they move to their permanent home in her new office. Miranda keeps files on every garden she's ever seen as well as useful articles and other information. "Everything is archived," she says. "That way if I'm working on steps in a garden, I can go to the file for 'steps' and see other garden steps from India to Ibiza." Friends reap the benefits of

Miranda's imaginative decorating at the casual suppers she holds at home. A charming container garden full of flowering trees and other plants graces the outside deck. Strung up high and lending the space a festive air are Chinese and Turkish lanterns and oversized colored Christmas tree bulbs. Sitting outside on cushions made from a blue and white fabric Miranda found in Mallorca, guests enjoy the simple meals she whips up herself. Miranda knows that decorating and gardening mean nothing without friendship. "In a way, the gardens I love to do most are the ones I've done for friends," she reflects, "because I get to see them grow and change and evolve."

Miranda, in a Jane Mayle dress, sits outside on her porch. The blue and white fabric on the cushions is a find from a summer holiday in Mallorca. The Turkish and Chinese lanterns are strung above the lush and blooming dianthus and honeysuckle.

Where would you like to live?
South of Spain.

Who are your favorite heroes of fiction?
I rather like Stendhal's icy Mathilde.

Who are your favorite heroes in real life?
Florence Nightingale.

Who is your favorite painter?
Diego Velásquez.

What is the quality you most admire in a man?
Knowing how to build a fence.

What is the quality you most admire in a woman?
Warmth and high spirits.

What is your favorite occupation?
Gardening, dancing, cooking—all the nice things.

Who would you have liked to be?
Talleyrand.

What is your most marked characteristic?
Dramatic mood changes.

What is your principle defect?
I take everything too seriously and I can't spell aloud.

What is your favorite color?
Pink and red.

What is your favorite bird?
The canary (I have to be loyal).

Jeanne and Gabriel, the two canaries,
in their wooden cage from Spain.

120

Above: Old photographs of bullfight and bullfighters from a market in Seville line the fireplace mantle in the living room.
Right: A watercolor master plan for a garden design by Miranda.
Below: Miranda on her way in from the garden.
Opposite: The bedroom. Curtains and bedspread of embroidered red poppies by Brigitte Singh. The film *The Red Lantern* was Miranda's inspiration for the whimsical lantern next to the chandelier.

ANDREW LAUREN

The table is set. Astrud Gilberto's voice floats sweetly from the speakers. It's a mild summer night and parents are on their way over for dinner on a tiny, postage stamp of a terrace. They are eager to see their son's new apartment. This is enough pressure to crack any child who's just stepped out of the nest—but imagine standing in the shoes of Andrew Lauren, son of Ricki and Ralph Lauren, builders of the Polo empire.

Andrew Lauren, an actor who recently founded his own film production company, happily accepts his father's style. This was not always quite so. He spent much youthful energy determinedly avoiding the Ralph Lauren look until he realized it was "no use fighting what was best." Indeed, today his apartment has the feel of an archetypal urban Ralph Lauren setting, full of sleek, well-made furniture and decorated with quirky antiques, vintage books, and other personal memorabilia that Andrew has been collecting for years.

"I love my father's style," Andrew admits. "But one thing that made me really proud was finding my own. When my father first walked in he said, 'I just don't know what you can do with this space.' But to me, this place felt like the Guggenheim-meets-1930s-producer's office. It was very simple, strong, and modern. There was something about the space that just felt sexy. The next time my father saw it, he flipped out. He loved what I'd done." From any father, that's a big compliment. From Andrew Lauren's father, it's practically a papal nod.

Like his father, Andrew has the ability to transform inspirations into something visible and new. "It makes me proud when people walk in here and ask me where I got something," Andrew says. "I hope I have a decent eye. I love to buy things at the flea market and put them back together myself. And then people come in and they think that I've gotten them from an expensive store." Andrew designed the bookshelves himself and in an interesting quirk arranges his books by color rather than subject or author. "I just found that when I came home I wanted everything to be simple. The randomness of book spines struck me as complicated, so one day I just decided to color-code them." He's not above making other changes to suit his own vision of the world. Upstairs in the bedroom, he's amassed an impressive collection of photographs and drawings. One recent purchase wasn't quite right, so he fixed it. "I bought a late 19th-century drawing of a nude woman reclining on a couch. It's so simple it feels like it could be modern. But it bothered me a bit that she looked kind of masculine. So I gave myself the liberty of redefining her breasts somewhat with a pencil. I know it's a travesty and I'm sure a lot of artists will hate me for doing this. But I wanted to make her more real for me." Andrew takes his love of vintage glamour one step further than most people. His business requires that he spend a lot of time in both New York and L.A., but he really hates to fly. His solution? He takes the train. "It takes about four days, if I stop in Chicago," he says. "I bring my computer. I catch up on books and music. I kind of disappear for a couple of days. It's nice to take your time for a change."

Previous page: A view of Andrew Lauren's architectural staircase. On the desk sits Andrew's favorite figurine, Batman. "Sometimes I like to think of my place as Bruce Wayne's pad."
Above: Andrew seated at his desk, with behind him Jean-Max poster designed by artist Paul Colin known for Josephine Baker's posters of the 1920s and 1930s.
Below: A corner of the bedroom. On the table, a bronze figure, "The Smoker," by J.C. Leyenbecker. The shelves hold photographs of the Kennedys, Gary Cooper, and Patricia Neal.
Opposite: A stainless steel cabinet from a kitchen supply store on Lafayette Street.
On top of the cabinet is part of Andrew's photographs collection, including a shot by Jacques Lowe of John and Jackie Kennedy's townhouse in Georgetown.
Next page: the living room as seen from the top of the winding staircase.

Where would you like to live?
Santa Fe or Capri.

What is your idea of earthly happiness?
Beautiful women, someone to love, a couple of close friends, creativity.

Who are your favorite heroes of fiction?
James Bond, King Arthur, Gatsby.

Who are your favorite heroes in real life?
My mother and father.

Who are your favorite characters in history?
John and Robert Kennedy, Che, Roosevelt, Steve McQueen, Gary Cooper, Cary Grant, Steve Ross.

Who is your favorite painter?
Fritz Scholder.

Who is your favorite musician?
The Beatles, 2 Pac.

Who is your favorite writer?
Fitzgerald, Hemingway, Faulkner, Kerouac.

What is the quality you most admire in a man?
Confidence mixed with humility.

What is the quality you most admire in a woman?
Support, patience, independence, intelligence, and ability to forgive.

What is your favorite occupation?
Driving.

What is your principle defect?
Never being happy with what I already have.

What is your favorite color?
White—you can always add to it.

What is your favorite bird?
Those "Cling Cling" birds in Jamaica.

AUDRA AND JASON DUCHIN

Blake and Mingus, two miniature Australian shepherds named after legendary musicians, greet visitors to the Broome Street loft of Jason Duchin and Audra Avizienis. Thelonius Monk plays on the stereo. In this apartment, the jazz aura seems especially appropriate, for Jason is the son of celebrated Society pianist and band leader Peter Duchin and grandson of the famous big band leader Eddy Duchin. After the death of his mother, Peter Duchin was raised by former New York Governor and United States Ambassador Averell Harriman. Harriman and his first wife Marie took Peter in on their estate near Tuxedo, New York. It's a rich family history, but one that has very little bearing on the current generation.

Jason, bohemian-looking with his ponytail and goatee, has found his own way, and seems entirely unconcerned with high society. Most of his waking hours are spent devoted to the DreamYard Project, the non-profit arts education initiative he founded seven years ago with partner Tim Lord. DreamYard's mission is to bring professional artists into schools that have no arts budget and incorporate art into the curriculum. The program currently reaches over 3,000 children in New York and Los Angeles.

Originally from Chicago, Audra Avizienis, of Lithuanian descent, was working in New York as a model when the two met at a party on a boat in the East River eleven years ago. After attending Columbia University, she went to work as a journalist and is currently a "head grammarian" at Condé Nast.

In the spring of 1995, the two decided to get married and began to hunt for a new apartment. After seeing some fifty spots, Audra found the space on Broome Street. "It was an amazing dump," says Jason. "There was even a glassed-in spa on a raised platform in the corner where everyone could watch you taking a shower. It was like a 70s love grotto." "It was hideous," Audra agrees. "But we knew we could do something with the space."

Their old lease was up, so Jason and Audra moved right into the construction zone. They set to work demolishing walls and reconfiguring the layout. Audra laid the tile in the bathroom. Jason sanded the floors and uncovered the brick walls and ceiling beams. One would never guess the original state. "It was a very intense six months," says Jason. "I think we knew that if we could get through that and still want to get married, then everything would be OK."

They both have many fond, albeit unusual, memories of hauling wreckage down to the street at midnight. The owners of Il Buco, a wonderful local tapas bar down the block, took pity on Jason and Audra and often invited them in for a glass of wine in the wee hours. In a sentimental gesture of gratitude, the Duchins held their wedding reception at the restaurant. At the time, the area was considered dodgy at best, but the move was prescient. Now dubbed NoHo, the neighborhood is the trendiest in the city.

The Duchins' apartment holds an eclectic mix of possessions. Walls are crowded with art lugged home from trips around the world: black-and-white prints picked from Audra's Lithuania, masks from Bali and New Guinea, figures from Thailand, ceramics from Mexico, and arrowheads from both Africa and Wyoming.

Commenting on the mix, Jason says, "I love watching people come in here—especially kids from DreamYard—and just start looking. The kids will go around and pick things up, open them, ask questions. I love seeing the reactions. It's great to see people interact with the space in a comfortable way."

"You can see that we don't necessarily worry about color coordination," adds Audra. "And we're not particularly caught up in 'style.' But we hope there's a sense of warmth and welcome here."

First page: Jason and Audra in the living room. Above the sofa are two photographs taken in Africa by Jason's sister Courtnay.
Previous spread: Jason and Audra's hands cast in plaster by a sculptor friend sit beside knives from Morocco and Kenya.
Opposite: Audra in a slip-covered chair in the entrance. Behind her, a collection of framed Lithuanian prints.

KAREN AND FERDINAND GROOS

"Only in New York," says Karen Groos, shaking her head, as she recounts the ordeal of apartment hunting. "We had to fly over from London to interview for it. And it's just a rental!" But the open lay-out and big windows that let in lots of light charmed her and her husband Ferdinand.

"At first, it was completely collegiate and basic looking," she remembers. "We put sisal carpet down and bamboo blinds on the windows and just moved right in with all of Ferd's English furniture. To be honest, it looked a lot like a suite at the Carlyle. That's when we decided to go for some color." The bold palette was inspired by a Christopher Giglio photograph which hangs in the living room. Giglio exposes photo paper by placing it in front of a television screen and turning on the power for a split second. The results look more like abstract paintings. Using that picture as a guide, they turned the completely white apartment into a series of yellow, orange, and red rooms. "It took some guts," says Karen. "But everything just fell into place from there. It looks best at night. The colors mellow and the rooms feel warm and cozy. The yellow is a bit too canary, but I'm living with it."

Karen and Ferdinand met while students at Brown University. Ferdinand was raised in Germany. Karen was raised in bohemian splendor in North Africa by her Lebanese father and Canadian mother, before going back to England for school. Her law career has been placed on the back burner while she stays home to care for their one-year-old son, Leopold.

Any cherished object can find a spot in the young cosmopolitan couple's informally chic apartment. A plastic Superman figure from the 1950s looks as if he's about to fly away from his perch atop the bookshelves in the dining room where Groos often hosts simple spaghetti suppers. Four watercolors by the illustrator Jean-Philippe Delhomme were a birthday present from Ferdinand. He calls the series, "Things to do when you turn 30": "Go see different cultures"; "Repaint your house in bizarre, vivid colors"; "Hang out with younger people"; and "Explore the stars". "He just found them and made up the theme," says Karen. "But it's great because I really did do all those things around the time I turned 30."

A red felt sofa in the living room was designed after the one in Coco Chanel's Paris apartment. "Ferd was adamant about having a sofa with just one seat cushion. No subdivision." The pillows are made from antique Persian textiles, a wedding gift. The foyer's own irrepressible whimsy is a mural of an enormous tree with sprawling branches. "Ferd and I had gone to Texas for the weekend for a wedding. Lizzie, a German friend, was house sitting and unbeknownst to us began to work on what she called *our* wedding present. She stayed up all night painting, while a friend read her bits of the Studio 54 book. She copied the tree from the fabric on the living room armchair. I guess most people would have been mortified when they got home, but when I was growing up I was allowed to doodle on one wall of my bedroom, so I absolutely loved it."

Interior designer David Netto, an old friend, arranged the disparate elements of their different worlds. "He has a superb eye," says Karen. "He'd probably be the first to disclaim this place. It isn't really

Previous page: Karen Groos, barefoot, kneels at the dining room table hard at work on her scrapbooks. Behind her, on the burnt orange color wall, a painting by Jean-Michel Basquiat.
Above: "Explore the stars," a watercolor by Jean-Philippe Delhomme next to a Superman figurine and an iron alligator doorknocker.
Left: Leopold Groos in a leather club chair. Below: "Paradise," a photograph by Jack Pierson next to a 1930s French lawyer's cabinet in the dining room.
Opposite: Karen stands in the doorframe between the living and dining room.

his style, but he helped us find pieces and figure out how to do things. Some of the stuff we have in the apartment David has lent to us, like the neo-classical console in the entrance and the big mirror that sits on top. When we couldn't find anything we liked, David generously parked some things with us. They're on indefinite loan, although he keeps sending us photos of things to look at because I think he wants his furniture back."

With its intense colors, wide-open space, and eclectic furnishings, the apartment feels almost exotic compared to most New York apartments. Karen credits that feeling to her childhood in Tunisia, where she lived in a cliff-side house overlooking the harbor of a small village. "Everything was so sensual," she remembers. "You could smell jasmine all the time. There were colorful Arabic tiles everywhere. The little iron balconies on houses were painted a beautiful light blue. Our house had a big palm tree growing out of the center courtyard, and my mother had decorated it all in total 1970s bohemian style—white shag throw rugs, geometric pattern curtains, big Nigerian leather poufs to sit on. Growing up there definitely gave me a love of color and the confidence that you could mix everything up and succeed." Only in New York, indeed.

Karen and Leopold on the red sofa Ferdinand designed after the one in Coco Chanel's home in Paris. Above them, a Christopher Giglio photograph, the colors of which inspired the bold scheme in Karen and Ferdinand's apartment.

What do you regard as the lowest depth of misery?
Hopelessness.

Where would you like to live?
Here, now.

What is your idea of earthly happiness?
Our son Leopold.

To what weaknesses are you most indulgent?
Inadvertent ones.

Who are your favorite heroes of fiction?
Howard Roarke, Die Budden Drooks, Andri
(*Andorra* by Max Frisch).

Who are your favorite heroes in real life?
Our parents.

Who are your favorite characters in history?
Napoleon, Churchill, Erhardt.

Who is your favorite painter?
Jean-Michel Basquiat.

Who is your favorite musician?
Always changing, but right now it's Manu
Dibango (a Cameroonian singer).

Who is your favorite writer?
Ferdinand: Max Frisch, Kafka, Thomas Mann.
Karen: Norman Mailer, John Updike, and
Honoré de Balzac.

What is your favorite virtue?
Integrity.

What is the quality you most admire in a man?
Courage, leadership, integrity.

What is the quality you most admire in a woman?
Humor, kindness, intelligence.

What is your favorite occupation?
Raising our son.

Who would you have liked to be?
A leader in the field of medicine.

What is your most marked characteristic?
Ferdinand: An independent spirit.
Karen: Curiosity.

What do you value most in your friends?
Loyalty.

What is your principal defect?
Ferdinand: Impatience.
Karen: Indecisiveness.

What to your mind would be the greatest of misfortunes?
Living through war.

What is your favorite color?
Ferdinand: Blue.
Karen: Shocking pink.

What is your favorite bird?
Ferdinand: The Concorde.
Karen: The ostrich.

Karen and Ferdinand Groos at the Frick Museum's Edwardian Ball.

SERENA ALTSCHUL

Serena Altschul anchors the news on MTV and hosts and produces several of the network' documentaries. With her signature short blond crew cut and fancy pink mules she found in Cyprus, Serena waltzes into the lobby of the building she will soon be calling home. And what a lobby it is. Her building is one of the few spectacular Art Deco buildings that line Central Park West. Several key members of New York's Mafia once called it home, too.

The building was completed in the 1930s and still retains much of its original Art Deco detail. Unfortunately, the Great Depression interfered with the architect's grand visions. The lower floors, built before the stock market crash, are full of rich artistic detail and expensive materials, but the upper floors, completed after the money started running out, are a bit more modest.

Serena had rented a place in her beloved West Village for several years. But when it came time to buy, she searched the entire city. "I looked at about 20 or 30 places," says Serena. "My mother was looking for me as well and we stumbled on this place in 'estate' condition. The owners were an elderly couple who were ballroom dancing champions. Trophies and plaques from ballroom dance-a-thons hung all over the walls and the apartment was decorated in '1920s faux French'," says Serena. "In addition to that, there was water damage everywhere." Today, the apartment is a complete construction site. "I am here everyday, everyday," says Serena. "I'm very detail oriented." Adament about being involved in the evolution of the apartment, she has worked out a new plan with a young architect, Amanda Brainerd.

Serena's apartment will be the result of several factors, borrowing elements from both her parents' apartments to create a retreat to which she can escape from the hustle of her job and the bustle of the city. When Serena was growing up, her mother lived in a very cool, modern apartment full of Swedish furniture, while her father, a well-known collector of Impressionist paintings, lived in a more traditional, turn-of-the-century-style apartment, full of reds and browns and silk painted walls. "My place will be a sort of hybrid," explains Serena. "I plan to have rich colors but just splashes of it, like in the bright red lacquered sliding doors in the media room. I'm often under bright lights in the studio, so I've put in cove ceilings with recessed lighting that will glow with soft, indirect light." The ceilings have all been dropped eight inches to house the elaborate lighting and electric system. "It's my nest in the sky," she says. "I feel like I can really breathe up here." The space where her bedroom will be has two large windows that look directly out over Central Park. "During construction, I've been able to watch a pair of nesting swans."

Serena's job, which often takes her into edgy, precarious situations, is what makes her long for a haven to come home to. She can spend up to six weeks in the field researching, writing, and producing pieces for her documentaries. Of late, she traveled to Arizona and Texas interviewing teenagers in order to do research for episodes on teenage use of heroin and crystal meth. Next, she heads to a

military base in North Carolina and is scheduled to parachute out of a plane in the middle of the night with 2,000 to 4,000 new Army recruits. Serena's distinctive beauty makes her instantly recognizable to fans all over the world, an entirely different kind of pressure. "I'm often in war-torn places—prisons, or maybe somebody's makeshift basement drug factory," Serena explains. "I investigate the grim reality of many teenagers' and other people's lives. I'm not in Mariah's limo or Puffy's boat; I'm in trailer parks. I look forward to having a place to escape from the dark world I inhabit professionally."

What do you regard as the lowest depth of misery?
High school—no wait, junior high school.

What is your idea of earthly happiness?
To live boundlessly and to contribute to other people doing the same.

To what weaknesses are you most indulgent?
Without a doubt, "toffutti cuties" at midnight.

Who would you have liked to be?
My friend Richard believes I'd like to be Harpo Marx, "the happiest man who ever lived."

Who are your favorite heroes of fiction?
Eloise, The Wild Things.

Who are your favorite characters in history?
I'll tell you when I'm older.

What is the quality you most admire in a man?
Is an ass a quality?

What is your favorite virtue?
Passion and compassion.

What do you most value in your friends?
Comfort, safety, laughter.

What is your principle defect?
Paranoia—why do I seem like I have a lot of defects?

A view of Central Park from Serena's Upper West Side apartment on the 30th floor.

A Bright Young Thing is not about being a socialite,
a big star, or the prettiest. Bright is what we give the
highest regard: intelligence, intuitive intelligence, street
smarts of the highest order. Boulevard smarts, in other
words. Bright Young Thing to me, is just positive,
positive, a win win.

JEFFREY BILHUBER

The world has changed, money has changed, style has
changed. America is so prosperous now. Money is
circulating in places much more than ever and it's good
for business; it's good for the couturiers, it's good for
the hairdressers, it's good for the florists. There's a
whole new generation that has taught itself to turn out,
a whole new attitude out there. I think it's great. I think
it's amusing. Just think of the Metropolitan Museum's
Costume Institute ball last winter. What a style evening
it was. That place really rocked. I thought, "Oh God,
Diana Vreeland, you must be enjoying it up there
tonight."

C.Z. GUEST

Style isn't about being fabulous or fashionable, but
about being comfortable in your own skin.
Get that right and everything else falls into place.

GRAYDON CARTER

America's most pervasive
age-related disease is not
senility but juvenility,
the obsessive desire to look
23, dress 14, and act 9,
avoiding responsibility and,
as Dr. Johnson put it,
hanging loose upon society.

TOM WOLFE

I hate white. White is not a color. People are so bigoted
about color. They're afraid of it. Colors are like people.
Some are more difficult than others. Anything's okay if
you do it the right way.
I never met a color I didn't like. Love thy colors.

RICKY CLIFTON
(whose favorite decorators are Twombly, Mondrian and Freud)

SLOAN LINDEMANN AND ROGER BARNETT

"Moroccan, Moroccan, Moroccan," mutters aloud Sloan Lindemann as she busily prepares for this evening's seated dinner for twenty in the dining room of the Park Avenue apartment she shares with her husband Roger Barnett. Clutching Lucy, her miniature Dachshund, Sloan surveys the room. "Lucy is the most spoiled dog I know," she coos. "She winters in Florida and flies private and eats only diet food—no scraps. Scraps can be the end of these dogs. Lucy lives more glamorously than most people I know!"

Dining room walls are painted with murals depicting Moroccan scenes in Marrakesh—the souk, camels, palm trees. "Someday we will have to move, but I will put a provision in the contract that no one can ever paint over the dining room mural," Sloan says. "Can you imagine having to be the painter hired to paint over this treasure? What a shame."

Sloan commissioned decorative artist James Smith to give the apartment a touch of exoticism, and tonight's Moroccan-themed dinner pays homage to the mural by pulling out all the stops. Glorious Foods, the famed caterer, has prepared courses of couscous and various tagines. Dinner will be served from authentic Moroccan clay dishes and serving pieces. The waiters will be perfectly costumed. Lanterns hang low from the ceiling and votives line the windowsills, casting the room in a perfect, dark glow. The low table brought in especially for this evening has been covered in orange silk. Colored pieces of crystal and amber are scattered across its surface. The guests will sit on cushions on the floor. It's a scene conjured up out of the *Arabian Nights*.

What's the occasion? "Nothing in particular,"

says Sloan. "It's just fun to have friends over to eat good food and drink good wine. And this was a really different way to do it."

Not all of the apartment is Moroccan in flavor. It's a mix of many styles, reached by consensus. "This was my apartment before we were married," explains Sloan. "When Roger moved in, some things just had to go! The bedroom was a bit too feminine for him, so the toile came off the walls and we made it less colorful. The office now has room for two. It can be difficult to find a style that makes you both happy. Everyone has an opinion—and my husband's can be especially strong. But it's been worth the bumps along the road. We love our apartment now." One thing certainly here to stay is a painting by Chagall, a bride and groom flying over the French countryside. "Roger gave it to me when we were engaged," explains Sloan, "and it's my favorite treasure."

"This apartment was not a job done in one fell swoop," explains Sloan, who enlisted decorator Janet Le Roy to work on the living room and library. "Janet is meticulous. Every last piece is an individual process and she must see everything in the context of the entire room before she approves. But once she's gotten it just right, you never want to move again." So where does the vase full of shocking pink ostrich plumes fit into this whole scheme? "The feathers were part of the centerpiece at our wedding," she sighs sentimentally. "I'm afraid someday they will just give out. 'No thank you,' they will say. 'No more.'"

The same will never be said, one predicts, of Sloan's own unflagging energy and determination. After graduating from New York University Law School, she worked as an assistant district attorney in Manhattan. A few years later, she left law to try her hand at broadcast journalism. These days, she co-hosts *She Commerce*, a cable network show produced by Oxygen Media. Her spirit is matched by her husband's entrepreneurial zeal. After stints in investment banking and perfume marketing, Roger founded Beauty.com last year. And both will have a new focus for their energy come September, when their first child is due. They've extended the mural idea from the dining room to the nursery, where the walls are painted with scenes from *Curious George*. "That's really our favorite room in the whole apartment now," Sloan says with a smile. "We're thinking of kicking the baby out and moving in."

First page: Sloan Lindemann Barnett and Roger Barnett in the living room.
Previous page: Sloan in costume with her "guardians" for the evening await guests for a Moroccan seated dinner party in the dining room.
Above: The dining room with its candlelit low table, Moroccan lanterns, and painted scenes of camels, tigers, and the souk.
Below: Place cards attached to tangerines for the evening's dinner.
Opposite: Twenty seated guests enjoy the authentic Moroccan fare.

SUSAN FALES-HILL

"I'm not into simplicity or minimalism and I'm not much of a modernist," states Susan Fales-Hill. "Can't you tell? This place is about anything but playing it safe." Certainly, a very bold personality had a hand in creating these rooms in striking palettes that range from deep red in the dining room to saturated blue in the study. Susan credits her verve to the "training of the divas," as she puts it. Her mother, Josephine Premice, was a famous Broadway actress and Susan spent her childhood surrounded by people in show business.

In 1958, Premice was appearing in a musical called *Jamaica* with Lena Horne when she met the Brahmin, Timothy Fales, of Boston. Their marriage a year later caused a scandal. Mixed-race couples were still a shock to American society. When a business opportunity offered the couple a chance to decamp for Rome, they jumped at it. "I think they were very happy to get away from the United States for a while," says Susan.

La Dolce Vita era was in full swing and famous people were passing through Rome all the time; Premice and Fales hosted each and every one of them. Burton and Taylor would pop by for surprise visits while they were filming *Cleopatra*. Premice had put her stage career on hold, choosing instead to build a household and start a family, and Susan and her brother were both born in the Eternal City. When Susan was two, the family returned to New York and Premice went back on stage. Susan had a front-row seat for her parents' theatrical coterie.

"My mother's friends were all of these incredibly glamorous, independent women like Diahann Carrol, Lena Horne, Eartha Kitt, and Carmen De Lavallade, one of the first black *prima ballerinas* in the world," Susan explains. "They were all way ahead of their time, unique,

controversial, fearless, and never worried about fitting in. More is more was their thing. Very Auntie Mame." Susan's mother was a character herself. "No one was quite the role model my mother was," says Susan. "She had the greatest imagination. Once, we were staying at the Ritz in Madrid. She was going out that evening and needed a pair of earrings to wear with her black taffeta dress. She looked up at the chandelier and suddenly snatched of a few of the crystals, and *voilà*! She still amazes me to this day."

After New York's Lycée Français and Harvard, Susan sent a writing sample to family friend Bill Cosby, who was impressed enough to give her an apprenticeship on *The Cosby Show*. When *A Different World*, starring Lisa Bonet, was conceived, Susan moved to Los Angeles to write for that show, making her way up to head writer and then executive producer. Susan married investment banker Aaron Hill and moved back to New York into Aaron's one-bedroom bachelor pad. She's hard at work on a new pilot for Showtime.

Living in a classic 1907 Park Avenue building, Susan considers the most important room to be the dining room, dramatically painted deep red with draperies and chairs covered in fabric of the same intense shade. An ornate antique silver chandelier that once hung in Toronto's Holt Renfrew department store lights the enormous round antique dining table. "I found the table before we were even married," says Susan. "My husband said, 'You don't even know where we're going to live yet.' But I had to have it. You don't find tables like that everyday." The chairs once belonged to Diahann Carrol, who gave them as a wedding present. A painting of Susan's great-great-great-grandfather painted by Gilbert Stuart hangs on one wall. It's a formal yet inviting space. And when the room is lit with the tiny oil lamps Susan uses at dinner parties, it glows softly. "It's a good place to linger," says Susan. "I'd never want to live anywhere without a dining room. I love to have people over and I love to cook for them. Dining rooms are special places. I just think it's uncivilized to eat in the same place where you lounge."

PLUM SYKES

New York loves a British tongue. Hard-boiled urbanites melt upon hearing those clipped consonants and precise vowels. Nowhere is this more true than in the fashion world, whose authoritative seasonal pronouncements go down so much more smoothly when uttered with a stiff upper lip. So, in her three years on American soil, Plum Sykes, a fashion writer at *Vogue* and a sort of English Holly Golightly for the 21st century, has found herself in the swirling heart of New York chic.

Every month her column, "Fashion Fiction," chronicles the foibles of the fabulous and reveals just which trend the in-crowd is swooning over. The column answers such questions as what to do with your suddenly un-chic pashmina wrap, whom to call to spruce up your Hamptons summer rental, and what new technological accessories notify you of incoming calls when the cell phone is tucked inside a handbag. After all, according to the column, "One absolutely must not be seen with phone out on table top, ever. Looks desperate."

It was the outrageous things Plum overheard during her nights on the town covering events for *Vogue* that gave her the idea for the column. Some comments were so ridiculous that she had to find a way to use them. Her two main fictional characters are constantly running into a gang that includes most of New York's bold-faced gossip column *habitués*. "Usually, they're all thrilled to be in it," says Plum cheekily. "But I have had a few complaints from socialites—apparently they don't like actually being called socialites."

Obviously, Plum Sykes isn't a girl who spends many nights at home with her hair up in curlers. Still, her tiny railroad flat on a quiet Greenwich Village side street is decidedly homey, and extremely understated. Consider the fact that she brought absolutely nothing with her when she moved here from London and you'll appreciate the achievement even more.

First thing, she painted the walls her signature lilac. The color seems perfectly appropriate for a girl named Plum, but she explains that it's become somewhat of a family tradition. The color first appeared in her grandmother's house, then her mother followed suit and now Plum's got the hue too. "A white room is the most boring thing in the world," says Plum. "Painting is the cheapest, easiest, fastest way to transform it."

Then came the furniture. "I spent every Sunday for six months at the flea market. And more time in and out of little vintage shops in the East Village. I like old-fashioned things best, and it's so small in here that big modern furniture wouldn't work, and expensive antiques would look ridiculous even if I could afford them. So, I just bought good inexpensive things as I found them. I didn't have chairs for months." All the wood surfaces of the furniture were slapped with a coat of white paint, which next to the springtime-colored walls gives the tiny apartment the feeling of a Cecil Beaton stage set.

As befits a fashion editor, Plum has a good eye and enjoyed using it at home rather than on her wardrobe for a change. "Obviously, this place is not about money. I think it's very young feeling, as if

The drama of a *frivolous* society is revealed only when its frivolities destroy that society's members.
— EDITH WHARTON

PARTY IDEAS.

* COCKtails @ 7 P.M.
& Dinner at 8 P.M.
* Awards @ 9:30 P.M.
Social security. business attire.
Cipriani's @ 42nd St right by
Grand central btw. Madison +
Park.

ANNA WINTOUR

Please R.S.V.P. to Lauren
as soon as possible.
Thank you.

Previous page: Plum braces an arm against the doorframe to her bedroom. The door has been replaced with a plastic gypsy bead curtain.
Top: A detail of Plum's desk with stacks of pink note cards used when researching columns for *Vogue*.
Opposite: A lazy morning for Plum in her plum colored bedroom.
Next page: A busy girl's refrigerator door. A cartoon of Plum, most prominent amongst photographs and invitations, drawn by fashion designer Spooky.

it's a girl playing dress-up in fancy old clothes. But it took imagination: something that might look really disgusting at a flea market could have excellent potential if only you know to look for it."

When it comes to clothes, Plum also likes old. She revels in mixing romantic vintage pieces with newer designer items in a style that she calls "bohemian attic chic." Quite clearly, the same term applies to her decorating sense. The philosophy is simple: find well-made items from an earlier era and fit them into your modern life.

Matilda Cecily Rock
March 11, 2000
7 pounds, 15¼ ounces

What do you regard as the lowest depth of misery?
Going off a boyfriend who hasn't gone off you.

What is your idea of earthly happiness?
Never going off a boyfriend who never goes off you.

To what weaknesses are you most indulgent?
Chocolate, fur, and cigarettes.

Who are your favorite heroes of fiction?
Aristocrats with issues: Lily Bart, Sebastian Flyte,
Mrs. Dalloway.

Who are your favorite heroes in real life?
Beautiful, talented, stylish women—Coco Chanel,
Nancy Lancaster, Lauren Hutton.

Who are your favorite characters in history?
Mary Queen of Scots, Anne Frank, and any woman
who survived marriage to Henry VIII.

Who is your favorite writer?
Social observers: Oscar Wilde, Henry James,
Truman Capote, Edith Wharton, Evelyn Waugh,
E.M. Forster, Kingsley Amis, F. Scott Fitzgerald.

What is your favorite occupation?
Holidaying following a stint of fruitful work.

Who would you have liked to be?
Julie Christie—I always wished I grew up in the
1960s.

What is your most marked characteristic?
My Englishness.

What do you most value in your friends?
Longevity—the longer I know them, the better they get.

What is your principle defect?
Seeing the funny side of everything except myself.

What to your mind would be the greatest of misfortunes?
Never falling in love.

LILLIAN WANG AND DAMIAN VON STAUFFENBERG

"Everything about this Michael Kors poncho had an enormous influence on the way our apartment looks today," says Lillian Wang von Stauffenberg, pointing to the shawl casually draped over a chair in the living room. Indeed, its simple, clean lines and color scheme—bold chocolate bands alternating with camel and a flash of orange—are repeated throughout the two-bedroom apartment she and her husband Damian share with their nine-month-old son Sebastian.

Fashion dictates Lillian's design sensibility—she has worked with and been influenced by some of the best names in the business: Calvin Klein, Michael Kors, and the legendary Dawn Mello. Recently, she was named Style Director at Verdura, the exclusive jeweler. Lillian credits all of these experiences with fine-tuning her eye, but she singles out two men as especially strong influences: Michael Kors, the fashion designer known for his classic American sportswear, and Richard Lambertson, whose line of handbags and accessories (created with partner John Truex) have become must-have items for fashionable women across the country.

Lillian and Damian perfectly represent the high end of the cross-cultural blend that defines New York. Lillian is Chinese-American. Her family left Shanghai in 1948 just before the Communist take-over. She was raised in Massachusetts, but speaks fluent Mandarin Chinese. Damian hails from an old, aristocratic German family. His childhood was spent between Risstissen, the family's castle in southern Germany, and Madrid, where his father currently lives. He is fluent in German, Spanish, French, and English. He has lived in New York

for three years and works as a private banker. Both love New York for its energy and glamour. "Everyone is an immigrant here," says Lillian contentedly. "It's hard not to feel at home."

Lillian loves to cook and has taught Damian a love of Chinese cuisine. On weekends, the two can often be found at the Chinese markets on Canal Street looking for Asian delicacies like fat and juicy Beijing pears and Dim Sum, the social Chinese tea-buffet traditionally eaten on weekend mornings. As far as food goes, there is only one thing that Damian misses in New York: a good German restaurant. "Whenever I'm longing for German food, I plan a business trip," he quips.

They have risen to the challenge of balancing their stylistic differences: Lillian's fashion sense and Chinese heritage and Damian's appreciation for the things he grew up with. A set of Louis XVI dining chairs co-exist peacefully with a Ming dynasty bench at the simple 19th-century French farmhouse table in their dining room. "We try to blend both modern and old," says Damian, "a little Chinese with a little European. By combining the two we can both be happy and feel at home."

What do you regard as the lowest depth of misery?
Damian: Traffic.
Lillian: Being apart from my family.

To what weaknesses are you most indulgent?
Damian: Food. Lillian: Shopping.

What is your favorite occupation?
Damian: Painting trees.
Lillian: Fashion designer.

Who would you have liked to be?
Damian: Caesar.
Lillian: Coco Chanel.

What is your most marked characteristic?
Damian: My nose.
Lillian: Stubbornness.

What is your favorite bird?
Damian: The penguin.
Lillian: The stork.

Who are your favorite characters in history?
Damian: Adenauer, Claus von Stauffenberg, Bismarck.
Lillian: Confucius, Jesus.

Previous page: Lillian Wang von Stauffenberg, dressed in head-to-toe white Michael Kors, perches on a Ming dynasty bench. The dining table is a French 19th-century farm table. Behind her is a painting by Huang She-Jing, a scholar in bamboo grove.

Above: Damian, Lillian and Sebastian. Left: Damian preparing Sebastian's bath. The painting above the tub was given to Lillian by Josephus Thimister, a designer for Balenciaga. Below: A Matisse drawing of a woman's profile above a stool upholstered in Hermès-orange suede.

AMANDA HEARST

"I am supposed to be on restriction right now," explains 16-year-old Amanda Hearst, a student at Choate-Rosemary Hall, the prestigious boarding school in Connecticut. "I had a boy in my room without permission and my punishment was that I couldn't go home for a month." Those are the rules, but this weekend Amanda was granted a reprieve. So she's enjoying her temporary freedom at home with her mother Anne Hearst in New York City.

Amanda is the great-great-granddaughter of George Hearst, the self-made multimillionaire rancher and miner whose prospecting ventures in the West led him to be a partner in three of the largest mining discoveries in United States Gold Rush history. The Indians called him "the man the earth talked to" for his ability to sniff gold. In 1880, he won a little newspaper, the *San Francisco Examiner*, in a card game. Since journalism didn't interest him much, he handed it over to his 23-year-old son William Randolph Hearst, Amanda's great-grandfather. That paper formed the cornerstone of the publishing empire that still bears the family name. Amanda's grandfather, Randolph Apperson Hearst, is the last of William Randolph's five sons still living and he continues to sit on the board of the Hearst Corporation. In addition to its many other media holdings, the family corporation today is also the world's largest publisher of monthly magazines, with a total of 16 American titles—including *Harper's Bazaar, Cosmopolitan, House Beautiful, Good Housekeeping,* and *Town & Country*—and a hundred international editions.

With a publishing empire in her family history, it is no wonder that Amanda has dreams to some-day join the business as a writer or fashion editor. "My mom's been an editor at *Town & Country* for years," she says. "I'm used to that lifestyle and that career." Right now, however, Amanda is busy being a teenager. Her idols are Michelle Pfeiffer, Gwyneth Paltrow, and Laetitia Casta, whom she calls "the greatest model of all time." She often dreams of Paris and travel abroad, and is as content as can be with her knapsack packed with blue jeans and "Juicy Couture" T-shirts from her favorite New York store, Scoop. She loves the color pink and collects fashion Barbies with designer clothes.

Her room at school is the ultimate reflection of her style: lots of flowers and, of course, pink. "After all the school dances, the boys give flowers. I've dried them all—hung them upside down and put them all over my wall," Amanda explains. "When I grow up and have my own house," she muses, "I'll try to decorate each room with a theme. My bedroom would be just like my room at school now, but with a big comfortable bed with lots of pillows. Milly de Cabrol, one of my mom's closest friends, would help me. She's a decorator with tons of style. Of course, I would have an enormous bathroom, all to myself, with a deep marble tub with water jets. I would love a really great kitchen, too. Not that I can cook, but I love food."

Until then, it's sushi with mom at her favorite Japanese restaurant down the street. "I never wear white to sushi," she says, sounding very much like the famous Eloise, as she skips out the front door.

What do you regard as the lowest depth of misery?
Chemistry class.

Where would you like to live?
New York City.

What is your idea of earthly happiness?
Eating cookie dough ice cream in my pajamas
watching *Days of our Lives.*

To what weaknesses are you most indulgent?
Chocolate.

Who is your favorite musician?
Lynyrd Skynyrd.

Who would you have liked to be?
Elizabeth Taylor, Michelle Pfeiffer.

What is your most marked characteristic?
My eyes.

What do you most value in your friends?
Humor.

What is your principle defect?
Short attention span.

What is your favorite color?
Pink.

What is your favorite bird?
The ostrich.

Previous page: A real Bright Young Thing, Amanda Hearst, 16, poses in
front of a Venetian framed portrait of her great-grandmother, Mrs. William
Randolph Hearst. The portrait was painted on the Hearsts' honeymoon in Paris.
Opposite: A bookshelf in Amanda's bedroom holds an old photograph of
the Hearst brothers: Bill; Jack; Amanda's grandfather, Randolph; and
David. A Frank Sinatra doll stands tall among the fashion plate Barbies.
Sinatra and Amanda's mother, Anne, were closest of friends. A watercolor
of Amanda painted in Monaco, a copy of *The Catcher in the Rye* and
Wuthering Heights, a pack of Juicy Fruit chewing gum and the Hearst family
christening coat are among Amanda's belongings.

TARA AND MICHAEL ROCKEFELLER

The Rockefeller name evokes many things: great wealth and power, of course, but also political involvement, arts patronage, public service, and philanthropy. Ever since John D. Rockefeller, Jr. started handing out dimes to children during the Great Depression, the family has been known for its many acts of public benevolence, especially in the area of the arts. In 1925, John D. Rockefeller, Jr. built and endowed The Cloisters, the romantic and dramatically-situated building in Fort Tryon Park which holds most of the Metropolitan Museum of Art's medieval collection. A few years later, his daughter-in-law, Abby Aldrich Rockefeller, helped found the Museum of Modern Art, forever linking the family's name with the patronage of serious contemporary art. Her son Nelson, who served as governor of New York in the 1960s and then as Vice President of the United States under Gerald Ford, turned the grounds of Kykuit, the family's estate on the Hudson, into a vast sculpture garden dumbfoundingly full of works by many of the 20th century's greatest artists. Nelson's son, Michael, spent years collecting the works from New Guinea and the South Pacific in the Met's holdings. In 1961, when Michael disappeared during one of his trips recording the art of the Asmat Papuans of New Guinea, one of the last surviving stone age cultures, Nelson, and the Rockefeller family, endowed the Met's Michael C. Rockefeller Wing. Tara and Michael (named for his lost uncle) are the latest in this line and their apartment is full of both family treasures and new ones they've collected themselves.

In 1937, Nelson Rockefeller had commissioned the great French furniture designer Jean-Michel Frank to decorate his Fifth Avenue apartment, one of only two commissions that Frank, whose work is now highly prized by collectors, received in this country. The apartment was legendary for the sleek, modern lifestyle it embodied. Michael and Tara were lucky to have been given many pieces from that apartment by Michael's grandmother, the late Mary Todhunter Clark Rockefeller, Nelson's first wife. Those pieces form the backbone of their collection. "Both Michael and I love furniture from that period," says Tara, pointing to a Macassar ebony desk that once sat in Nelson's office. "The simple forms, beautiful materials, and proportions work with every age and culture." Indeed, the apartment that Michael and Tara share with their two young children is a precise study in harmony. Modern and Oriental art coexist with the 1930s furniture. "Michael has a genius for hanging things and combining radically different styles," says Tara. Michael has carried on the family tradition of collecting, while managing to indulge his other interests at the same time. Youthful indecision may have fostered this Renaissance-man attitude: after majoring in art history at Dartmouth, he attended the Harvard Business School, then proved his membership in the computer generation by starting his own Internet advertising company, Active Media.

But Michael is a Rockefeller, and art is in his blood. He collects photography and is an amateur photographer himself. He has cultivated a keen interest in new, up-and-coming artists and tells the story of "discovering" artist Elizabeth Peyton at an art fair: "Almost all her work had been sold before the fair had even opened. She paints on glass, not canvas, and had run out of available glass to work on. I was living Downtown at the time and a tenement building across the street was being demolished. So I piled six or

seven large pieces of glass from the building onto the ski rack of my car and lugged them down to her studio."

Tara traveled extensively in Asia before her marriage, picking up treasures along the way. "With all the mix of periods and provenances in our apartment today, my mother calls our decorating style 'Early Attic, Late Cellar,'" says Tara with a laugh. The apartment itself is full of stories—it was once home to another famous furniture designer, the architect George Nelson. Their building, incorporated in 1883 as the Gramercy Family Hotel, is the oldest surviving cooperative apartment house in the city and the first to have an elevator (hydraulic-lift) in a residential building. "Stepping into the lobby, with its dark wood paneling, original stained glass, and mosaic tile floor is like going back in time," says Tara. Best of all, just across the street sits Gramercy Park, a tiny green oasis in the middle of the concrete city. The apartment's impeccable address is matched by the Rockefellers' furnishings. A Jean-Michel Frank-designed parson's table even has an old-fashioned pencil sharpener screwed to the top. "Someone in the family must have been hard at the homework years ago," jokes Michael. Even though so much New York history surrounds them, Michael and Tara are truly of this age.

Below: An Elizabeth Peyton portrait painted on a glass window pane hangs over a Jean-Michel Frank desk designed especially for Michael's grandfather's, Nelson Aldrich Rockefeller, famous salon at 810 Fifth Avenue. Giacometti designed the pulls and the burgundy leather is Hermès. Opposite: Michael and Tara at the dining room table in front of a four paneled leather painted screen by Victor White with folkloric scenes from Oyster Bay Long Island's sound and beach.

Above: Michael and Tara on a bench in Gramercy Park. The bench bears a plaque with the name Mary French, whose son was Nelson Rockefeller's roommate at Dartmouth College.
Below: The fireplace designed in renovation by Michael and Tara references the Deco form throughout the apartment. The small side chair beside the fireplace is Jean-Michel Frank. A Toby Khan painting hangs above the mantle.
Opposite: The living room seen over two Tang dynasty terracotta horses and the dining room table. The dining room chairs belonged to Nelson who had them made in California. The large mountainscape in the background, "Magian Way," is by Yolanda Shashaty.

LULU DE KWIATKOWSKI

Lulu de Kwiatkowski is one of those rare birds who is able to translate their inner vision of the world into a physical space. On walking into her 2,000-square-foot apartment in a staid Upper East Side building, one sees how successful she's been. The space is full of intense hues and geometric patterns. Moorish-style arches connect rooms and set off tiny plush alcoves that could be hiding places in a pasha's palace.

Lulu, a native New Yorker, was always drawn to the art of other cultures, especially Morocco, India, and Peru, for their sense of color and rhythmic abstraction. She went to Parsons School of Design to study fine arts and painting, but soon switched to interior design. "Limiting myself to one small, square canvas was too intimidating," she recalls. "I had too many ideas to cram into such a little space, I needed to work in a bigger environment. As I get older, I'm getting more comfortable with my ideas, and the act of painting on a canvas is getting easier." Some of her own paintings hang on the apartment walls and the rest were painted by her brother Stephan, who has a similar love of color.

The youngest of the six children of Henryk de Kwiatkowski, a Polish immigrant and the famously self-made horse-breeder, Lulu wanted more than be that season's "It" girl. She packed herself off to Paris for five years where no one knew nor cared a whit about her family. There, at school, she found a way to combine her loves of color, geometry, and painting. She studied *trompe-l'oeil* and eventually apprenticed with the Italian master, Francesco Gurnari.

When she resurfaced on the New York scene, two years ago, she launched Lulu DK Fabrics, a decorative painting company; her clients' walls radiate with colors seeped in geometric and floral designs. Lulu DK

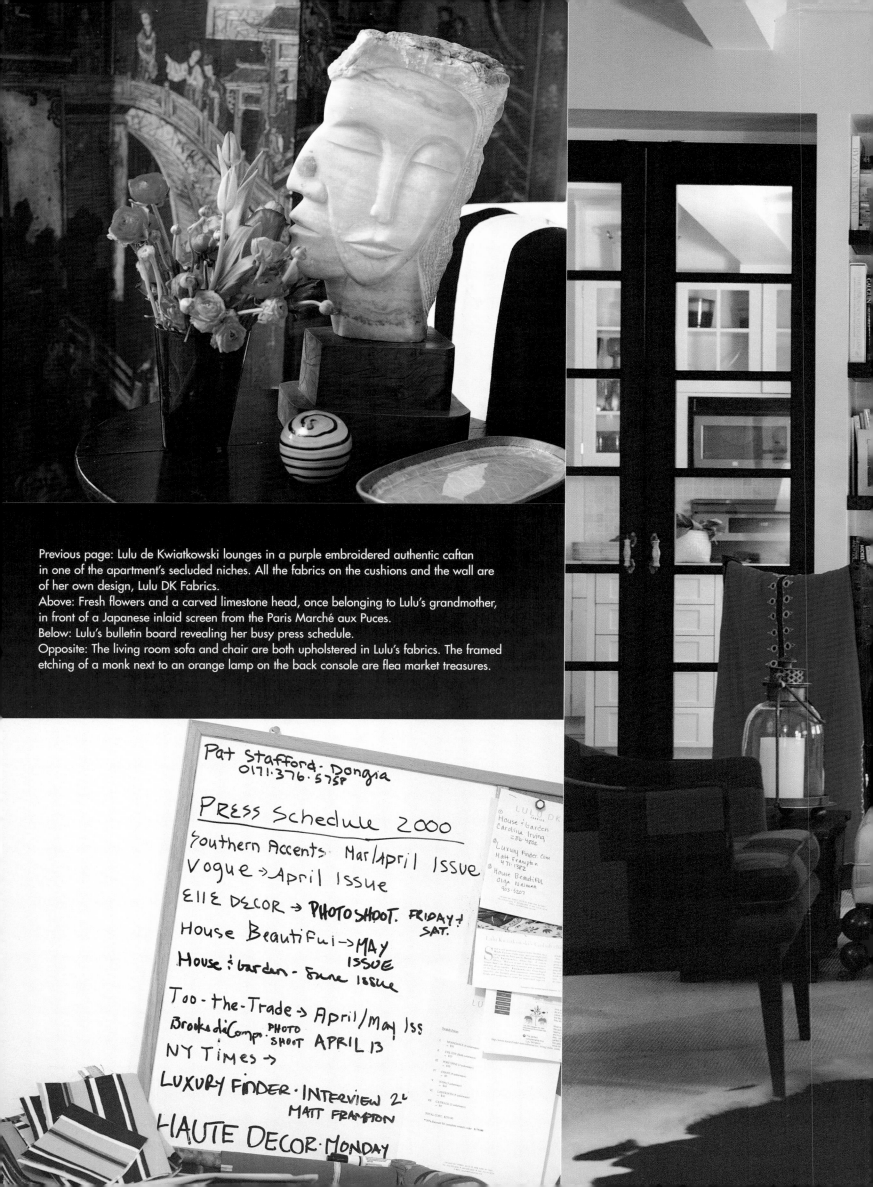

Previous page: Lulu de Kwiatkowski lounges in a purple embroidered authentic caftan in one of the apartment's secluded niches. All the fabrics on the cushions and the wall are of her own design, Lulu DK Fabrics.
Above: Fresh flowers and a carved limestone head, once belonging to Lulu's grandmother, in front of a Japanese inlaid screen from the Paris Marché aux Puces.
Below: Lulu's bulletin board revealing her busy press schedule.
Opposite: The living room sofa and chair are both upholstered in Lulu's fabrics. The framed etching of a monk next to an orange lamp on the back console are flea market treasures.

Fabrics uses some of the same sophisticated patterns in a new line of textiles which are currently littered in swatches all over her home office.

W, Vogue, and *The New York Times* Sunday Styles section clamor to get her photo into their pages, but Lulu is ambivalent about their fawning. She seems happiest when working at home in a pair of jeans, with some background music to keep her company.

The previous owner had lived in the apartment since 1932 and it needed a lot of work. "I knew exactly what I wanted to do with my place the minute I saw it in its original disastrous state. I had looked at a hundred apartments," she recalls. "They were all Downtown, and I didn't really want to look up here at all. But the agent convinced me that I had to see this one, and I bought it on the spot." Lulu had the place gutted and started building from scratch. The front hall is dominated by grand gestures: a paint scheme of squares of various shades of one color layered on top of each other, a red lacquered ceiling, a zebra rug on the floor, and a Moorish arch leading into the living room. The tiny details consume her; delicate Limoges porcelain pillboxes have turned into doorknobs. Most of the furniture comes from New York's 26th Street flea market. "I'm there every weekend," Lulu says. "I'm very much a hunter-gatherer, and I'm always looking for something else to bring home. Truth be known," she admits, "I change my apartment more than I change my clothes."

The possibility of a ghost in the apartment just adds more color and charm: "I think the former owner is still around," laughs Lulu. "But she seems nice, so I don't think she hates the change. And she keeps the mice away."

Left: Lulu's office at home covered with fabric swatches from her new line.
The whimsical wrought iron chair is from the flea market on 26th Street.
Next page, left: Lulu's charming interior scape watercolor of her apartment.
Right: Lulu in one of the Muslim arches she designed for doorways.
Last spread: Lulu's kitchen. The painting to the right is by her brother Stephan.

What do you regard as the lowest depth of misery?
A hangover with no juice.

To what weaknesses are you most indulgent?
Coffee and cigarettes, which I quit a year ago.

Who are your favorite heroes of fiction?
Superman, of course. I could always use him around the house!

Who are your favorite heroes in real life?
Superman, of course. I could always use him around the house!

Who are your favorite characters in history?
Amelia Earhart.

Who is your favorite painter?
Rothko, Balthus, Stephan (my brother).

Who is your favorite writer?
Kay Thompson.

What is the quality you most admire in a man?
Sanity.

What is the quality you most admire in a woman?
Grace.

What is your favorite occupation?
Artist, archaeologist, geologist, writer, historian.

Who would you have liked to be?
Myself, five years from now, with longer legs.

What do you most value in your friends?
An ability to understand myself.

What is your principle defect?
Bad spelling.

What to your mind would be the greatest of misfortunes?
A sky without sun.

Of late, it's impossible not to notice that style is in the air again, after a long dormant period. The young people I see around New York wear evening clothes wonderfully well, look sophisticated, and are fiercely involved in their careers. It's a new kind of style, and a very welcome one.

DOMINICK DUNNE

Thank Heaven for pretty girls,
They grow up in the most delightful way.
Thank Heaven for pretty girls
and the handsome men who steal their hearts away.
Thank Heaven.

SLIM AARONS (singing)

It could be a Southern Belle's cluttered boudoir or a study in empty elegance. Everyone creates their own fantasy, a cocoon to protect them from the fast, brash, loud, and exhilarating urban landscape that is Manhattan. The city's most successful interiors suggest that style is about having the courage of your convictions, and that it embraces both good and bad taste. After all, as that quintessentially stylish New Yorker Mrs. Vreeland declared, bad taste is better than no taste!

HAMISH BOWLES

All girls are beautiful, but New York girls like the "Bright Young Things" in these photographs are also talented and smart—which make them the most beautiful of all.

FRANK ZACHARY

With enormous appreciation and thanks to:

Billy Norwich, for the title and for hanging in from start to finish; Frank Zachary, for his invaluable time and for dreaming up the cover; Slim Aarons, for his inspirational work; Graydon Carter, for his loving mockery; Dudu von Thielman, for her encouragement; Tom Cashin, for his advice and friendship; Christopher Cerf for his dark room; Charlie Churchward; Shax Riegler; Hannah Thomson, for her patience and expertise with lights, cameras and the car; Jolie Hirsch, for her persistence; Dorothée of Assouline, for everything, but mostly for keeping peace; Stephanie, for being so willing; Amanda and Lili, for holding down the fort; and mostly, for Robert and Linda Douglass, who know why.

Those who gave of their wits and wisdom:
Slim Aarons, Brooke Astor, Jeffrey Bilhuber, Bill Blass, Hamish Bowles, Graydon Carter, Ricky Clifton, Bob Colacello, Anh Duong, Dominick Dunne, C.Z. Guest, Carolina Herrera, Eleanor Lambert, Marian McEvoy, Oscar de La Renta, Andre Leon Talley, Tom Wolfe twice and again, Frank Zachary.

Everyone photographed in the book, for their trust, support, and patience. Most of all, for their enthusiasm.

Credits: Hannah Thomson assistant to Jonathan Becker; Michael Gabor and L&I Color Laboratory; Sarah Jenkins Black and White Laboratory; Nucleus Imaging (NYC); Green Rhino Color Print Laboratory; Tuleh; Christian Dior; Glorious Foods; Bill Tansey Designs; Party Rentals; Paul Podlucky, the hair and make up genius.